AF600504

# INVALIDITY OF DISPENSATIONS ACCORDING TO CANON 84 § 1.

THE CATHOLIC UNIVERSITY OF AMERICA
CANON LAW STUDIES
No. 340

# INVALIDITY OF DISPENSATIONS ACCORDING TO CANON 84, § 1.

A HISTORICAL SYNOPSIS AND A COMMENTARY

A DISSERTATION

*Submitted to the Faculty of the School of Canon Law of the Catholic University of America in Partial Fulfillment of the Requirements for the Degree of Doctor of Canon Law*

by

STANISLAUS J. KUBIK, S.T.D., J.C.L.
Priest of the Diocese of Worcester, Mass.

THE CATHOLIC UNIVERSITY OF AMERICA PRESS
WASHINGTON, D. C.
1953

NIHIL OBSTAT:

EDUARDUS G. ROELKER, S.T.D., J.C.D.
*Censor Deputatus*

Washingtonii, D.C., die 16 februarii, 1954.

IMPRIMATUR:

✠ JOANNES J. WRIGHT, S.T.D.
*Episcopus Wigorniensis*

Wigorniae, die 23 februarii, 1954.



THE HEFFERNAN PRESS
WORCESTER, MASS.

# TABLE OF CONTENTS



## PART I

HISTORICAL SYNOPSIS

## PART II

### CANONICAL COMMENTARY

## FOREWORD

The Church as divinely instituted by Christ is a juridically perfect society. It possesses the means through which all its members may eventually attain the perfect end, namely, eternal salvation. As in any perfect society, so also in the Church, the *conditio sine qua non* through which its existence is more or less assured is Authority. This authority in the Church is empowered to make laws according to which the society is governed and according to which its members live in peace and harmony. Laws, however, are more often than not rather rigorous, and their application in all cases allowing no relaxation whatever regardless of any peculiar and totally justifiable circumstances, would create hardship both on the society as a whole and on its members as individuals.

Realizing this, the Church, a provident Mother, at times permits a relaxation of the law in particular cases whenever the causes justify it. This relaxation is called a *Dispensation.* Such relaxations from the general norms or ecclesiastical laws are not granted indiscriminately, nor could they be. No law is made without some reason, and thus, also, its relaxation must be made in accordance with reason.

The purview of this treatise takes into consideration only the tenets of canon 84, § 1, namely, that a dispensation from an ecclesiastical law, when granted by a subordinate dispensing agent without a just and reasonable cause, is illicit and invalid. Since the jurisprudence concerning this question was not established overnight, the first part of the treatise will deal with the early centuries of the Church's history in so far as the author and the accepted causes for dispensations are concerned. It was only with the era of the decretalists that the question of a subordinate's authority in dispensations was expressly considered. Thus a study of the early history will show how the jurisprudence evolved and finally emerged with an almost unanimous acceptance of the doctrine that a subordinate dispensing authority cannot validly dispense from the laws of a Superior without a just and reasonable cause. This doctrine was officially incorporated into the Code of Canon Law in canon 84, § 1.

The second part will be concerned chiefly with the analysis of the quality of the causes required for a dispensation, as called for by canon 84, § 1. Whatever other canons may be invoked, they are used merely as examples; an exegesis of each canon is not intended. The term *dispensation* is considered only in the strict sense, namely, as denoting a relaxation from the law in a particular case; consequently the dispensation *super rato*, from vows, and from vindicative penalties, is given no formal consideration.

The writer takes this opportunity to express his gratitude to His Excellency, the Most Reverend John J. Wright, S.T.D., Bishop of Worcester, Mass., for the opportunity to pursue graduate studies in Canon Law at the Catholic University of America; to the members of the Faculty of the School of Canon Law for their unselfish assistance and encouragement; and to all those who have aided in any way in the preparation of this dissertation.

# CHAPTER I

## PRELIMINARY NOTIONS

### Article 1. Concept of a Dispensation

Dispensation in the Code of Canon Law has a very precise meaning which had undergone a definite evolution during the early ages of the Church. The present day concept of *dispensation* has been codified in canon 80, which states that it is a relaxation from the law in a particular case. It is said to be a relaxation, since it suspends the obligation of the law in a given case for the good of the subjects. Since it takes an act of jurisdiction to grant a dispensation, this relaxation from the law can be made only by the legislator, his successor, or his superior, and also by an agent to whom the faculty to grant dispensations has been conceded.[1] A just and reasonable cause is required by law generally for a relaxation of any legislation.

Since the dispensation may be granted only by the lawgiver, by his successor or his superior, or by his delegate, and since a human lawgiver for the Church is herein intended, the law from which a relaxation can be given by the aforementioned is a positive ecclesiastical law, either universal or particular. The pope as the supreme legislator for the entire Church has the power to dispense from all ecclesiastical laws, even though there are certain ecclesiastical laws from which the Roman Pontiff is not wont to grant dispensations, although, strictly speaking, he has the power to do so. His jurisdiction, however, does not extend to natural law, nor to the positive divine law; consequently, neither he nor any other human authority can dispense from the laws of God.[2]

The relaxation is made in a particular case, but this does not postulate that it must be a favor which is granted to one individual, since it can be, and often is, granted to a group in a special case. In this way a dispensation differs from an abroga-

[1] Canon 80.

[2] Cf. Van Hove, *De Privilegiis; De Dispensationibus* (Mechliniae-Romae: Dessain, 1939), nn. 379-381.

tion of the law. An act of abrogation revokes the law completely, whereas a dispensation leaves the law unchanged and it indeed remains operative. A dispensation simply suspends the obligation of the law for this particular case, while retaining its full vigor and application for all other instances.

A dispensation differs from all other juridic institutes which, although similar in some respects, nevertheless evince basic distinctions between them. Thus a dispensation is not the same as:

1. *Interpretation,* which declares that a certain case does not come under the tenets of this particular law: in other words, it declares that in this instance the law does not obtain. This is not an act of jurisdiction exercised by the author of the law or by his delegate.[3]

2. *Epikeia,* which is a private and benign interpretation that the law does not obtain in a particular case. It does not in the least change the objective obligation of the law; rather, because of the peculiar circumstances, it excuses from the moral obligation in the internal forum, though the action thus performed involves a material violation of the law. Epikeia does not entail a positive act of jurisdiction of the lawgiver or of his delegate, but reflects the prudent subjective judgment of an individual.[4]

3. *Absolution from censures,* which is not a relaxation of the law but rather its application, since the law employs absolu-

[3] Cf. Michiels, *Normae Generales Juris Canonici* (2. ed., 2 vols., Parisiis—Tornaci—Romae: Desclée et Socii, 1949), II, 679 (hereafter cited as *Normae Generales*); Van Hove, *op. cit.,* n. 337; Rodrigo, *Theologia Moralis Fundamentalis,* T. II, *Tractatus de Legibus* (Santander: Sal Terrae, 1944), n. 446, 1 (hereafter cited as *De Legibus*); Cicognani-Staffa, *Commentarium ad Librum Primum Codicis Iuris Canonici* (Vol. I, Romae: Ex Officina Typographica Romana "Buona Stampa", 1939; Vol. II, Romae: apud Custodiam Librariam Pontifici Instituti Utriusque Iuris, 1942), II, 571 (hereafter cited as Cicognani-Staffa; Coronata, *Institutiones Iuris Canonici* (editio altera, Taurini: Marietti, 1939-1947), I, n. 108, a.

[4] Cf. Michiels, *op. cit.,* II, 680; Van Hove, *op. cit.,* n. 338; Rodrigo, *op. cit.,* n. 446, 2; Suarez, *Tractatus de Legibus ac Deo Legislatore,* Lib. VI, c. 10, n. 1—*Opera Omnia* (ed. nova a Carolo Berton, 26 vols. in 28, Parisiis: apud L. Vivès, 1856-1861), Vol. VI, p. 46 (hereafter cited as *De Legibus*); Coronata, *op. cit.,* I, n. 108, b.

tion as a means to remit the penalty after the necessary conditions have been fulfilled by the contumacious person. It presupposes a violation of a law, whereas a dispensation tends to forestall the transgression of the law by relaxing it in a particular case.[5]

4. *Permission,* which is in accordance to the law, since some acts are not prohibited by law, but the action cannot be placed without the consent of the Superior or of his delegate; this consent is postulated as a condition by the law itself. The law is in no way relaxed, nor is jurisdiction absolutely necessary in the giving of the permission as it is in the granting of a dispensation. Any legitimate authority can be empowered to give a permission, but not a dispensation. A permission may at times be presumed, whereas a dispensation cannot.[6]

5. *Dissimulation,* by which a Superior does not relax the law, but tends to ignore or overlook the obvious violation, since it would be difficult or impossible to insist on the observance of the law, or inasmuch as some greater evil would result from the insistence upon the observance of the law. Those who are guilty of such a violation of the law are usually not prosecuted in the external forum by the Superior.[7]

6. *Privilege,* by which the Superior establishes a special norm, which need not be contrary to the law, whereas a dispensation does relax the law in a particular case. Even privileges which are contrary to the law differ from a dispensation, inasmuch as they substitute a new objective norm in its place.[8]

## Article 2. Power of Jurisdiction

It requires an act of jurisdiction to grant a dispensation. The power of jurisdiction, however, can be either ordinary or

[5] Cf. Rodrigo, *op. cit.,* n. 447, 3; Coronata, *op. cit.,* I, n. 108, d.

[6] Cf. Vermeerch-Creusen, *Epitome Iuris Canonici* (3 vols., Mechliniae-Romae: Dessain; Vol. I, 7 ed., 1949; Vol. II, 6 ed., 1940;. Vol III, 6 ed., 1946), I, n. 187, d; Rodrigo, *op. cit.,* n. 448; Michiels, *op. cit.,* II, 681; Van Hove, *op. cit.,* n. 333.

[7] Cf. Van Hove, *op. cit.,* n. 335; Michiels, *op. cit.,* II, 680; Rodrigo, *op. cit.,* n. 449; Coronata, *op. cit.,* I, n. 108, f.

[8] Cf. Van Hove, *op. cit.,* n. 339; Michiels, *op. cit.,* II, 682; Rodrigo, *op. cit.,* n. 449, 2.

delegated. Ordinary power of jurisdiction is attached by law itself to an office; delegated power is that which is committed to a person.[9] Ordinary power of jurisdiction is by law attached automatically and with stability to an office. This power may be either proper or vicarious.[10] It is said to be *proper* when it is obtained by virtue of an office and is exercised in one's own name, not in the name of another; it is said to be *vicarious* when it is exercised by virtue of an office whence the power flows, but in the place of or in the name of another person.[11]

Vicarious power differs from delegated power inasmuch as vicarious power is proper to the office, whereas delegated power, having no connection with any specific office is conceded to a person in order that he may act with the authority of another. This concession of power may be made either by law or by man. Thus the one having *ordinary* power, whether proper or vicarious, is considered as the Superior, while the one possessing *delegated* power is to be considered as a subordinate who acts with the authority of the Superior.

Similarly *derived* jurisdiction differs from delegated jurisdiction. It is true that all delegated jurisdiction in the Church is derived, but not all derived jurisdiction is a delegated one. Thus, for example, the power of the Roman Pontiff is derived from God, but it is an *ordinary* power, whereas in many instances the power of the bishop is derived from the pope in the form of delegation.[12]

## Article 3. Ecclesiastical Law

Ecclesiastical law is a regulation in accordance with reason, promulgated by the head of the ecclesiastical community for the sake of the common welfare.[13] The law as proposed by the

[9] Canon 197, § 1.

[10] Canon 197, § 2.

[11] Cf. Coronata, *Institutiones Iuris Canonici,* I, n. 278; Vermeersch-Creusen, *Epitome Iuris Canonici,* I, 271.

[12] Cf. Wernz-Vidal, *Ius Canonicum,* II (ed. 3, a P. Aguirre, S.I., recognita, Romae: apud Aedes Universitatis Gregorianae, 1943), 427-428.

[13] Cf. Wernz, *Ius Decretalium* (3 ed., 6 vols., Prati, 1913-1915), I, 89, II: "Lex ecclesiastica . . . ordinatio rationis ad bonum commune ab eo, qui communitatis ecclesiasticae curam habet promulgata".

legislative authority of the Church can be a restatement or an interpretation of the natural and positive divine law, and as such it is to be considered rather as divine law than as ecclesiastical law in the strict sense of the term. On the other hand, the Church can propose human laws which as enactments exist distinct from and outside of the positive divine law, but are in strict harmony with the natural divine law. It is this positive human law which will be the object of this study.

The Church, as any juridically perfect society, certainly must have the legislative power by means of which it can formulate rules and regulations by which its members can be governed. Since the Church is a visible and temporal society whose primary end is to lead its members to salvation, it necessarily possesses the right to legislate concerning the spiritual as well as the temporal means which are necessary or at least useful in fulfillment of its formal purpose of existence. This legislative power of the Church is vested in the Holy See,[14] which has the governing power over the Universal Church, and also in other subordinate legislative authorities, e.g., in the bishop, who has governing power over his particular diocese. The Supreme Legislator for the Universal Church, however, is the Supreme Pontiff,[15] and his supreme power of jurisdiction emanates from divine law.[16] The pope's legislative power is exercised not only by means of the promulgation of the *Codex Iuris Canonici,* but also through the employment of any other means at his disposal to enact and promulgate laws for the Universal Church, as for example, a Papal Constitution. Nor is the pope restricted when he legislates to do so *per seipsum;* he may empower the various Roman Congregations to enact and promulgate laws for the Universal Church.[17] Still another source of universal legislation stems from the Oecumenical Councils,

[14] Cf. canon 7, which states that this term includes not only the Roman Pontiff, but also the Congregations, Tribunals and Offices which the pope uses to transact the normal business of the Universal Church.

[15] Cf. canon 218.

[16] Canon 219.

[17] Cf. Cicognani, *Ius Canonicum* (Romae: Ex Officina Typographica, 1925), n. 45.

provided that the decrees are approved and promulgated by the Supreme Pontiff.[18]

Besides this power of the Holy See to legislate for the Universal Church, there exists the provision in law for particular ecclesiastical legislation. Each ordinary[19] may enact and promulgate laws for his own territory or for his subjects, provided, of course, that they are not contrary to the general law of the Church. Such laws can be enacted either in a synod or even outside a synod by the local bishop for all his non-exempt subjects. The bishops of a particular territory, with due permission from the Holy See, may unite in a Plenary Council to legislate for their territory or provinces; or they may unite in a Provincial Council to enact laws for a particular province. Such particular laws upon review and recognition from the Holy See and after promulgation, bind all those whose domicile is within the territory for which the laws were enacted.[20] Others who are empowered to enact particular laws for their subjects in the Church are the Major Superiors of Religious Orders.[21]

Ecclesiastical law is positive human law, and as such depends upon the will of the legislator for its existence. So also does it depend upon the power and the will of the legislator for its abrogation in relation to all the subjects, or for a relaxation in some particular case without the abrogation of the law itself.[22] Canon 84, § 1, is concerned with dispensations from ecclesiastical laws, both universal and particular. Although all human laws are subject to a dispensation, nevertheless some of the ecclesiastical laws, because of their intimate connection with the natural law, do not fall within the category of laws which become the object of a dispensation. The subject matter

18 Cf. canons 227 and 228; to date there have been twenty such Oecumenical Councils.

19 Cf. canon 198, for those who are included within the scope of the term *ordinary*. However, the vicar general is not to be included as having power to legislate.—Cf. Cicognani-Staffa, I, 133.

20 Cf. canons 290-291.

21 Cf. canons 448, 8°, and 198, § 2.

22 Cf. Suarez, *De Legibus,* lib. VI, can. 10, nn. 2-4—*Opera Omnia,* VI, pp. 46-47.

of these laws is of such grave importance that it should not be called upon to suffer a dispensation.[23] Other laws are relative to faith or morals, and thus regard the public commonweal of the Church; from these laws the Church is not wont to grant dispensations.

Among the laws which are not subject to a dispensation in view of their initimate connection with the divine law are: 1) the impediment of *ligamen* arising from a valid existing bond of marriage on the part of Christians, when it has been consummated through the conjugal act;[24] 2) the impediment of antecedent and perpetual impotency;[25] 3) the impediment of consanguinity when there is a doubt whether consanguinity is in any degree in the direct line or in the first degree of the collateral line.[26]

There are some purely ecclesiastical laws from which, however, the Church does not grant dispensations at all, or from which the Church dispenses only very rarely. The Church will never grant a dispensation from: 1) the impediment of consanguinity in the first degree of the collateral line;[27] 2) the impediment of affinity in the direct line arising from a consummated marriage;[28] 3) the impediment of Sacred Orders arising from the episcopate, and almost never when arising from the priesthood;[29] 4) the impediment of crime in the event that with the co-operation of a third party, one spouse is the culpable cause of the death of the other spouse.[30]

23 Cf. Michiels, *Normae Generales,* II, 691-692.

24 Cf. canons 1069 and 1118; Rodrigo, *De Legibus,* n. 458; Gasparri, *Tractatus Canonicus de Matrimonio* (ed. nova ad mentem Codicis Canonici, 2 vols., Romae: Typis Polyglottis Vaticanis, 1932), n. 1126 (hereafter cited as *De Matrimonio*).

25 Canon 1068.

26 Canon 1076, § 3; Gasparri, *De Matrimonio,* n. 702; Cappello, *De Sacramentis,* Vol. V (6 ed., Taurini - Romae: Marietti, 1950), n. 525; Chelodi, *De Matrimonio* (5 ed., a Pio Ciprotti aucta, Vicenza; Società Anonima Tipografica Editrice, 1947), n. 98.

27 Canon 1076, § 3; Chelodi, *De Matrimonio,* n. 98.

28 Canon 1043; cf. also Gasparri, *De Matrimonio,* n. 722; Chelodi, *op. cit.,* n. 102.

29 Canon 1072; cf. also Gasparri, *op. cit.,* n. 619; Chelodi, *op. cit.,* n. 85.

30 Canon 1075, § 3; cf. also Gasparri, *op. cit.,* n. 683; Chelodi, *op. cit.,* n. 94.

This treatise, then, will not be concerned with these laws which are in practice *indispensabiles,* but rather only with such laws from which the Church customarily grants dispensations.

### Article 4. Meaning of the Term "Inferior"

The term *inferior* as used in canon 84, § 1, designates any dispensing agent who is neither the legislator, nor his successor, nor the superior of the legislator, but one who has the faculty to grant dispensations from the laws of the superior legislator through proper derived power or delegated faculties. Since this canon is concerned with purely ecclesiastical laws, the *inferior* therein specified is such in relation to ecclesiastical laws only. The Supreme Pontiff, then, is in no way an *inferior* in relation to any ecclesiastical law,[31] whereas all those who are in any way delegated by the Holy See or by the general law itself, as well as those who are empowered to grant dispensations from the general laws of the Church by means of derived ordinary powers, are included within the scope of the term *inferior,* which designates all those who are subordinates in authority.

#### *Section A. In relation to the general law*

All who are not included under term *Holy See* must be considered as subordinate dispensing agents in relation to the general law of the Church. Their powers for granting dispensations are regulated by canon 81, whereby all ordinaries who rank below the Roman Pontiff cannot dispense from the general laws of the Church, not even in a particular case, unless this faculty is conceded them either explicitly or implicitly. This canon concedes the power for dispensing provided that recourse to the Holy See is difficult and there is danger that grave harm will result from delay, and the dispensation is one which the Holy See customarily grants.[32]

Within the category of those who are *inferiors* in relation to

[31] I.e., in the sense explained in the preceding Article.

[32] Cf. Cappiello, *De Ordinariorum Dispensandi Facultate ad Normam Can. 81,* The Catholic University of America Canon Law Studies, n. 323, (Washington, D.C.: The Catholic University of America Press, 1952), for a detailed study of this canon.

the general law of the Church are those to whom, even though they are not ordinaries, is extended in one way or another the faculty to grant dispensations in specified instances, under specified conditions in certain definite laws: 1) pastors, when they dispense in virtue of canons 1245, §1, 1044 and 1045, § 3; 2) confessors, dispensing in virtue of canons 990, § 2, 1044 and 1045, § 3; and 3) local superiors of exempt religious when dispensing their subjects in virtue of canon 1245, § 1.

### *Section B. In relation to particular law*

The Holy See may enact laws not only for the Church universally, but, as the Supreme Legislator, also for a particular territory or even for a definite diocese. These laws, although particular in nature, are nonetheless papal legislation, and the local ordinaries cannot dispense except under the tenets of canon 81.[33] Consequently, the local ordinaries dispensing from this particular law must be looked upon as *inferiors* in relation to it.

Other particular laws are enacted in a Plenary or a Provincial Council, and, in relation to these, all the ordinaries within the territory for which these laws were enacted must be considered as *inferiors* in jurisdiction in relation to these laws. They may dispense validly from such decrees only in a particular case and for a just cause.[34] This includes the archbishop or the metropolitan, since he too is an *inferior* in relation to the laws of a Provincial or a Plenary Council.[35]

Each residential bishop is empowered to legislate for his own diocese. This he can do by means of synodal law, or through various decrees he may issue. He may grant dispensations from his own laws since he is the legislator, but he must do so in accordance with canon 84, § 1. The vicar general, when dispensing from the synodal law of his diocese, even though he is not the legislator he is nonetheless equivalent to

[33] Canon 82: Episcopi aliique locorum Ordinarii dispensare [nequeunt] in legibus quas speciatim tulerit Romanus Pontifex pro illo peculiari territorio, nisi ad normam can. 81.

[34] Cf. canon 291, § 2.

[35] Cf. Van Hove, *De Privilegiis; De Dispensationibus,* n. 376.

the bishop of the place[36] and as such he has the power to grant dispensations validly from the particular law of the diocese even without a just cause. This dispensation, however, would be illicit, just as would be the dispensation of the local bishop. Should the legislator deem it fitting, he could extend the faculty to grant dispensations from the synodal law, and those who received such delegated powers would in fact be *inferiors* in relation to the particular law of the diocese. Such delegation is generally given to the members of the Diocesan Curia upon whom the bishop depends to transact the normal business of the diocese.

The constitutions of the various Religious Orders are also particular ecclesiastical law for the members. The Superior General is the successor as it were, of the legislator in relation to the constitution, and is not a subordinate in relation to it. In the exempt as well as the non-exempt clerical Religious Orders and Institutes, the provincials and the local superiors are to be considered as *inferiors* whenever they grant dispensations from the decrees of the constitution of the Order or Institute in accordance with the faculties granted them by the Superior General or by their respective constitutions.[37]

[36] Cf. canon 198, §§ 1 and 2.

[37] Cf. Van Hove, *op. cit.*, nn. 422-426.

# PART I

# HISTORICAL SYNOPSIS

# CHAPTER II

## DISPENSATIONS TILL THE NINTH CENTURY

### Article 1. Existence

The early Church demanded a rather rigorous observance of the existing laws, which, in fact were few in number. It is not surprising that a relaxation from the general laws of the Church was a rare exception.[1] As a consequence the authors during the early days of the Church, saw no necessity to treat of dispensations expressly in their works. This seems to be the plausible explanation why no one ventured to formulate a juridical definition of a dispensation prior to Rufinus (c. 1157). And yet, in spite of the fact that the juridic institute of *dispensation* received no *ex professo* treatment, one cannot conclude that dispensation was an unknown entity to the early jurists.

Dispensations in the strict sense of the term, as accepted juridically today, namely, a relaxation of the law in a particular case,[2] were actually granted by the popes and bishops. This can be readily seen from the various examples of dispensations granted during the first five centuries of the Church;[3] and also from the writings of the Greek and the Latin Fathers of the Church.[4] Some of these dispensations in the early Church were granted *post factum*,[5] and some, though considerably fewer in number, were granted *ante factum*.[6]

[1] Cf. Thomassinus, *Vetus et Nova Ecclesiae Disciplina* (Magontiaci, 1786-1787), Pars 2, Lib. III, c. 24.

[2] Canon 80.

[3] Cf. Thomassinus, *op. cit.*, Pars 2, Lib. III, c. 24.

[4] Cf. Brys, *De Dispensatione in Iure Canonico* (Brugis: Beyaert, 1925), pp. 11-15.

[5] Cf. Thomassinus, *op. cit.*, Pars 2, Lib. III, c. 24, nn. 7-8; Mansi, *Sacrorum Conciliorum Nova et Amplissima Collectio* (53 vols. in 60, Parisiis, 1901-1927), II, 435 (hereafter cited as Mansi).

[6] Pope Gelasius (494) granted dispensations *ante factum* to the bishops of Italy, so that the interstices for the conferring of Orders could be passed over during the time when there was such urgent need of priests as a result of the ravages of war. — Mansi, VIII, 37; and also c. 1, D. LV; Jaffé, *Regesta*

This brief summary will suffice to show that dispensations actually did exist and were recognized in the juridical structure of the early Church, and that dispensations were not an innovation of the later centuries, when they were given some closer scrutiny during the time immediately preceding the *Decretum Gratiani.*

## Article 2. Author

The authors who admit that dispensations were granted during the first three centuries of the Church, unanimously agree that the bishops were the sole authors of dispensations.[7] This can be attributed to the fact that general ecclesiastical laws were few in number—that is, besides those set down in the Scriptures or in Apostolic Traditions, from which it was unlawful to grant dispensations. Whatever positive legislation existed in those early days was that which was enacted by the bishops themselves. Consequently, as legislators, the bishops had the power to dispense from their own laws in accordance with the principles of jurisdiction.[8] These laws were chiefly concerned with the reconciliation of penitents, the qualifications for Holy Orders and the remission of ecclesiastical penalties.[9]

Authors who busied themselves with the historical aspect of Canon Law gave various reasons in their effort to justify the powers assumed by the bishops to grant dispensations from general laws during the first three centuries of the Church's existence. Thomassinus explained the power of the bishops as a necessity of the times, since the bitter persecutions would hardly permit any recourse to the Holy See, or even consultation with other bishops, to say nothing of convening in Pro-

*Pontificum Romanorum ab condita Ecclesia ad annum post Christum natum MCXCVIII* (ed. 2 correctam et auctam auspiciis Gulielmi Wattenbach curaverunt S. Loewnfeld, F. Kaltenbrunner, P. Ewald, 2 vols., Lipsiae, 1885-1888), n. 636 (hereafter cited as Jaffé).

[7] Cf. Thomassinus, *op. cit.,* Pars 2, Lib. III, c. 24, n. 14.

[8] "Omnis res, per quascumque causas nascitur, per easdem dissolvitur."—c. 1, X, *de regulis iuris,* V, 41.

[9] Cf. Stiegler, *Dispensation, Dispensationswesen, und Dispensationsrecht im Kirchenrecht* (Mainz, 1901), pp. 14 and 73 (hereafter cited as *Dispensation*).

vincial Councils.[10] Febronius, whose writings are imbued with anti-papal teaching, advanced the opinion that episcopal power emanated from the power of binding and loosing which every bishop possesses and which extends even to the canons universally accepted by the Church. The reason for this, he claimed, was to enable each and every bishop to rule the diocese over which he was constituted, as it were, by the Holy Ghost.[11] Esmein explained the power of the bishops to dispense by claiming that it was connected with the fulness of disciplinary jurisdiction possessed by the bishops.[12] In fact there was only one avenue of action open for the bishops, which they used, although rarely: they simply granted dispensations from the law of the Superior. Stiegler followed the reasoning of Thomassinus, accepting the explanation that the bishops granted dispensations from the law of the Superior and he called this power *proper,* but only in the sense that recourse to the Superior was almost impossible. This power was joined to the episcopal office in so far as the bishop's power to rule his diocese is divinely granted.[13]

The doctrine concerning the origin of the power of the bishop to dispense from the universal law of the early Church is still obscure. Nevertheless, even though no early documents have been found which give conclusive proof to the theory of Thomassinus, it appears reasonably secure to follow his theory, namely, that this was brought about by the conditions existing in the early Church.

When a period of peaceful existence finally became the good fortune of the Church in the early part of the Fourth Cen-

10 "Cum acerbitas persecutionum, nec cum sede Petri communicare consilia fere sineret, nec episcopos alios adiri, nec concilia celebrari provincialia." —*Vetus et Nova Ecclesiae Disciplina,* Pars 2, Lib. III, c. 24, n. 14.

11 "Defluit haec potestas ex iure ligandi et solvendi quod cuivis episcopo datum est, et quod etiam exercet respectu canonum ab universali ecclesia acceptorum, tanquam a Spiritu Sancto positus, ut in sua dioecesi regat Ecclesiam Dei." —*De Statu Ecclesiae et Legitima Potestate Romani Pontificis* (Bullioni, 1765), I, c. 5, § 5, n. 3.

12 Cf. *Le Mariage en Droit Canonique* (2 ed., mise à jour par R. Génestal et Jean Dauvillier, 2 vols., Paris: Libr. de Recueil Sirey, 1929-1935), II, 359.

13 Cf. *Dispensation,* pp. 77-78.

tury, it also brought about a change in the juridical system of the early Church. Now the bishops, no longer restrained by the persecutions, were able to meet in provincial synods and enact legislation for their respective provinces. The popes, too, enacted laws for the universal Church. Thus a three-fold authorship for dispensations emerged, namely, the pope, the provincial synod, and the bishops: because as lawgivers, they could grant dispensations from their own laws.

From this period of the Church's existence, documentary evidence shows that the power of the Synod was superior to that of the individual bishop. This is shown by the various councils which at times granted powers of dispensation to the bishops of the Province, so that they, as delegates, could grant dispensations from the laws of the Provincial Synods.[14] The synods and the bishops acknowledged the power of the popes and furthermore accepted it as superior to their own. One example of this is the request sent to Pope Hilary (461-469) by the bishops gathered together in the Council of Tarracona, that he permit the transfer of Irenaeus to the see of Barcelona. The petition for this dispensation was denied by the Pope,[15] but the action of the Council gives added evidence to the fact that not only could the pope grant such a dispensation, but also that the Council acknowledged the superior power of the pope and abided by the decision. Quite often, nevertheless, bishops and synods usurped the power to grant dispensations from laws even when this was expressly prohibited them by the popes or the synods.

The popes through their decretal letters limited the right of the bishops to dispense from the general laws of the Church. Pope Siricius (385-399) forbade the bishops to grant dispensations to those who were undergoing penance, or those who had entered into second legitimate and valid marriages and after the dispensation sought to be admitted to Holy Orders. He warned that a penalty would be imposed on the

[14] Council of Ancyra (314), can. 2 — Mansi, II, 514; Council of Hippo (395), can. 2 — Mansi, III, 919.

[15] Cf. Mansi, VII, 926-928.

bishops who dared to act contrary to this prohibition.[16] Pope Gelasius I also cautioned the bishops lest they dispense without first obtaining permission from the Holy See.[17] The bishops recognized this power of the popes as superior to their own: more and more often they sought dispensations from the popes rather than rely upon their own powers. From the Ninth Century, the popes expressly vindicated for themselves the exclusive right to dispense from universal laws, and this right was acknowledged by the general councils. The bishops were not allowed to deviate from the canons, but they were to apply to the Holy See for any dispensation.[18]

## Article 3. Causes

Although there is a difference of opinion among the historians of Canon Law regarding the author, concept, and the manner of dispensations, they are in accord when it comes to the necessity of a cause or a reason before a dispensation could be granted. The legislator enacted laws for the common good, and in order that a relaxation from this law could be granted, it is logical that he required a justifiable reason why the law should not have been applied in its full vigor in a given case. Such relaxation of the law could not be left to the arbitrary application of any individual bishop. Such action would have imperiled the common good. In order, then, to allow a relaxation from the general law in cases where observance of the law was difficult or even opposed to the common good in a particular case, a just cause was required. Wherever a dispensation is recorded during the first nine cen-

16 "Scituri posthac omnium provinciarum summi antistites, quod si ultra ad sacros ordines quemquam de talibus bigamis et poenitentibus crediderint assumendum, et de suo et de eorum statu, quos contra canones et interdicta nostra provexerint, congruam ab Apostolica Sede promendam esse sententiam." —Mansi, III, 661; Jaffé, n. 255.

17 "Neque pro suo libitu episcopi jura studeant aliena pervadere absque sedis Apostolicae justa dispositione mandante."—Mansi, VIII, 38; Jaffé, n. 636.

18 Cf. Thomassinus, *Vetus et Nova Ecclesiae Disciplina,* Pars 2, Lib. III, c. 24, nn. 3-7.

turies of the Church, the necessity of a cause for a relaxation of the law in a particular case can also be found. A cause of necessity or benefit was not enough, only common necessity or benefit of the Church was considered as a sufficient cause.[19]

Thus, for example, Pope Innocent I (414) in his letter to the Bishops of Macedonia relaxed the law and permitted those ordained by the heretic Bonosius to be received into the Church in the same Orders in which they were constituted by ordination. While stressing the point that laws are to be obeyed and preserved, he nevertheless conceded that necessity of the times and the good of the entire Church merits such a relaxation. He followed immediately with the warning that as soon as the necessity ceased, the relaxation of the law ceased as well.[20] Pope Gelasius I also required a cause of necessity for the Church in general before the decrees of the canons could be relaxed.[21] Pope Martin I (649), moreover, reaffirmed that the popes are the "defenders and custodians of the divine canons" and refused to grant a dispensation for private benefit.[22]

Even though certain popes forbade bishops to grant dispensations and threatened them with penalties should they act contrary to these decrees, no indication was given in their decretals as to validity of the action of the bishops.[23] When a dispensation was granted without a cause of common necessity or benefit, a reprimand was given to the dispensing agent, but no inference was made as to the validity or lawfulness of such a dispensation.

Since the concept of dispensations was not fully developed during this period, it is not surprising that no regulation concerning the conditions for valid dispensations were enacted. It was only toward the end of the Ninth Century that the

19 Cf. Thomassinus, *op. cit.*, Pars 2, Lib. III, c. 24, n. 2.

20 Cf. Mansi, III, 1061; Jaffé, n. 303.

21 Cf. Mansi, VIII, 37; Jaffé, n. 636.

22 Cf. Mansi, X, 810; Jaffé, n. 2064.

23 V.g. Pope Siricius. Cf. Mansi, III, 661; Jaffé, n. 255.

question of lawful grants of dispensations by a subordinate dispensing agent arose. Even then it was not so much a question of a lack of a cause, it was rather a lack of jurisdiction on the part of the subordinate authority when dispensing from the law of his superior that was taken into consideration.

## CHAPTER III

## DISPENSATIONS FROM THE TENTH CENTURY TILL GRATIAN

During this period of the Church's history, the most satisfying factor, at least from the jurists' point of view, was the genuine effort to assemble methodical collections of law. An attempt was made to verify the laws and eliminate the spurious texts which so frequently found their way into various collections. Although this was not entirely successful, the progress which actually resulted from these efforts is gratifying. The doctrine on dispensations received a definite and even *ex professo* treatment in the works on Church law. Prior to the Tenth Century, dispensations received only a cursory examination usually bound up with the doctrine on reconciliation of penitents.[1] The progress made during this era is shown to good advantage in the *Decretum Gratiani* and in the Decretals.

### Article 1. Author

With the coming of the Gregorian reform, the emphasis was placed upon a centralized authority vested in the pope. The authors attributed to the pope the right to grant dispensations from the general law of the Church since he was recognized as the universal legislator. The one notable exception to this was Hincmar of Rheims who denied the right of the popes to dispense from the canons of the General Councils.[2] Perhaps the greatest exponent of papal power over dispensations during this era was Bernaldus of Constance. He attributed a special right to the pope to grant dispensations without, however, claiming exclusive papal rights to dispense. He considered legislative power of the pope as the basis for this papal prerogative.[3]

[1] Cf. Brys, *De Dispensatione in Iure Canonico,* p. 43.

[2] Cf. *Epistola III ad Synodum Suessionensem* — Migne, *Patrologiae Cursus Completus,* Series latina (221 vols., Parisiis, 1844-1855), CXXVI, 50 (hereafter cited as *MPL*).

[3] Cf. *De Statutis ecclesiasticis sobrie legendis* — *Monumenta Germaniae*

In practice, the popes reserved certain dispensations to themselves by limiting the powers of the bishops. This brought about more and more frequent appeals to the Holy See for dispensations. Some of the popes delegated the right to grant dispensations to the bishops, as, for example, Pope Paschal II (1107) granted Anselm of Canterbury the power to grant dispensations.[4] The Councils also denied the bishops the power to grant dispensations in certain cases, and even imposed penalties on those who usurped this power. The Council of Clermont (1130), under penalty of excommunication forbade the bishops and abbots to grant dispensations permitting their clerics to study civil law or medicine for personal gain.[5] The Council of London (1138) reserved to the Roman Pontiff the power to dispense in the cases of clerics ordained by a bishop, other than their proper Ordinary, unless the proper Ordinary issued dimissorial letters for them.[6] It became more and more apparent from the writings of the authors of the period immediately preceding the *Decretum,* that the universal right of the popes was vindicated; they based their assertions on the fact that the pope was the supreme lawgiver for the universal Church.[7]

In spite of the fact that the popes vindicated their right as the exclusive dispensing agents by limiting the authority of the bishops, not all the bishops of this period recognized this right of the popes. The authors who favored the reform were naturally interested that the supreme authority of the popes be vindicated, whereas those who opposed any reform in the Church's government bemoaned the fact that the bishops were being shorn of their rightful authority. Due to this contro-

*Historica, Libelli de Lite* (3 vols., editi a G. H. Pertz, Hannoveriae, 1891-1897), Tom. II, pp. 139-141.

4 *Epistola CCXXI ad Anselmum:* "Caetera etiam quae in regno illo pro necessitate temporum dispensanda sunt, juxta gentis barbariem, juxta ecclesiae opportunitates sapientiae ac religionis tua solicitudo dispenset."—*MPL,* CLXIII, 219; Jaffé, n. 6152.

5 Cf. canon 5 — Mansi, XXI, 436.

6 Canon 7 — Mansi, XXI, 512.

7 Cf. Brys, *De Dispensatione in Iure Canonico,* p. 66.

versy amongst the authors of this era, it is difficult to determine the exact relationship between the powers of the pope and those of the bishops, at least in so far as dispensations were concerned. Anselm of Lucca (born circa 1036) seems to deny the bishops the power to grant dispensations from the decrees of the Holy See.[8] Bernaldus gives an indication of this confusion when he first denied the bishops the power to dispense from universal laws of the Church, and in another passage conceded them this very same power. He tempers the latter stating that this is true only when the canons concede this power to the bishops.[9]

This same confusion is found in practice as in the theories proposed by the authors of this period. Very often the bishops would petition the Holy See for dispensations, at times requesting very broad faculties to dispense.[10] On the other hand, certain bishops could not see their way clear to submit to the idea that the popes had exclusive power and right to dispense from the universal law. As a matter of fact, they actually granted dispensations in matters expressly prohibited them by law.

### Article 2. Causes

This period is characterized by a marked confusion regarding the causes which were deemed as necessary for a grant of a dispensation. The more important authors of the era demanded a cause of common necessity or a cause of benefit to the entire Church, but in practice dispensations for private causes were granted. Abbo of Fleury (945-1004) enumerated causes which had to be taken into consideration before a dispensation could have been granted. He contended that for the common benefit of the Church many things were changed and tempered. Then he proceeded to give an exam-

8 "Nemo praesumere audeat temperare rigorem legis divinis, vel praescriptionum Sanctae Sedis."—*Monumenta Germaniae Historica, Libelli de Lite,* Tom. II, Lib. I, c. 20, p. 310.

9 Cf. *Monumenta Germaniae Historica, Libelli de Lite,* Tom. III, Lib. II, *de excommunicatis vitandis,* pp. 141-143.

10 Cf. Anselm's letter to Pope Paschal II, *Epistola XLII*—*MPL,* CLXIII, 191.

ple of a dispensation which was granted for the cause of a private nature, namely, the transfer of a certain Bishop Sylvanus, who because of human frailty could not withstand the cold winters of Philippopolis in Thrace and was assigned to the see of Troy.[11] Burchard of Worms (c. 1012) related transfers of bishops as permitted for the common benefit and necessity, and not at some one's pleasure; he illustrated this with examples, v.g., the transfer of St. Peter from Antioch to Rome, made for the common benefit of the Church.[12]

Among the principal authors of this era, Ives of Chartres (1040?-1116) was perhaps the major exponent treating *ex professo* concerning dispensations. He spoke of causes for which dispensations were granted and seemed to demand at all times a cause of common necessity or utility of the Church.[13] Due to the confused situation in regard to dispensations during this period, Ives at times seems to lean toward the idea of dispensations being granted for private causes.[14] Others who were either contemporaries of Ives or who preceded the *Decretum Gratiani,* followed the doctrine of Ives very closely. With the possible exception of Alger of Liége, the authors demanded a cause of common necessity and utility before they would admit that the cause was sufficient for a grant of a dispensation. They rejected a private good as a reason, even though they were aware of the fact that dispensations were granted in a particular case for a private cause.[15] This confusion amongst the authors seems to indicate that an evolution in the doctrine on dispensations was

11 "Unde considerandus est terrarum situs, qualitas temporum, infirmitas hominum, et aliae necessitates rerum, quae solent mutare regulas diversarum provinciarum. Potestate enim multa sunt pro communi utilitate ecclesiarum, quae nemo reprehendit fidelium. . . . Transmigratio episcoporum prohibita est in Nicaena et Chalcedonensi synodo; necessitate et utilitate concessa est in Antiocheno concilio. Et necessitate quidem propter frigus scilicet quod ejus debile corpus ferre non poterat, Silvanus ab Attico ex Philippopoleos in Trojam mutatus est."—*Collectio Canonum,* c. 8—*MPL,* CXXXIX, 481.

12 Cf. *Decretum,* Lib. I, c. 77—*MPL,* CXL, 569.

13 Cf. *Prologum in Decreto*—MPL, CXL, 569.

14 Cf. *ibid.,* pp. 51, 58.

15 Cf. Brys, *De Dispensatione in Iure Canonico,* p. 53.

actually taking place during this era. Practice differed from theory, for in practice dispensations for private causes were *de facto* being granted by the popes.

In his *Decretum,* Gratian followed the doctrine of Alger of Liége (c. 1121) who in his *Liber de Misericordia et Justitia,* proposed the causes required for a legitimate grant of a dispensation. Alger taught that dispensations may be granted for various reasonable causes.[16] He listed some of the causes for which dispensations could be granted and among them he gave: necessity of the times, various circumstances, and, in favor of an individual.[17] He also cited the evident merits of an individual as a cause for a relaxation of the law in certain cases.[18]

St. Bernard of Clairvaux (1091-1153), however, seemed to retrench by demanding the cause of common necessity or benefit for a legitimate dispensation; he did not consider private benefit as a sufficient cause for a relaxation of the law.[19]

The doctrine concerning dispensations during this period was not yet clear in respect to the effect that a cause had on the validity or lawfulness of a particular dispensation. Whenever the question of lawfulness arose, it was traceable not to the probable lack of a cause but rather to the probable lack of jurisdiction on the part of the bishop. Certain types of dispensations were reserved by law to the pope, as the supreme authority. Even so, in practice, certain bishops granted dis-

16 "Praeceptum vero quamvis sit omnibus necessarium, pro variis tamen rationalibus causis, ex auctoritate canonica persaepe est relaxandum."—*MPL,* CLXXX, 861.

17 Cf. *ibid.,* 861.

18 Cf. *ibid.,* 864.

19 *Liber III, de Consideratione,* c. 4: "Ubi necessitas urget, excusabilis dispensatio: ubi utilitas provocat, dispensatio laudabilis est. Utilitas, dico, communis, non propria. Nam, cum nihil horum est non plane fidelis dispensatio sed crudelis dissipatio est."—*MPL,* CLXXXII, 769. In a footnote (39) attached by John Mabillon, one finds the following: "Bernardi in materia dispensationum sententia: nempe ut nonnisi necessitate urgente, et communi utilitate suadente dispensetur. Jam vereor saepius dispensari, ubi necessitas et utilitas vel non est, vel tantum privata est." Thus it seemed even further established that theory and practice differed widely on this point.

pensations ordinarily reserved to the Holy See. Those who granted dispensations without a cause of common necessity but only for a private cause were reprimanded, but their acts were not declared null and void.

# CHAPTER IV

## DISPENSATIONS FROM GRATIAN TILL THE COUNCIL OF TRENT

Due to the *Decretum,* Canon Law emerged and developed as a science distinct from moral theology. This development was of great benefit to the science of Canon Law because it brought about a more detailed study of the various juridical entities; ecclesiastical laws were considered in greater detail and the juridic treatment of dispensations took on new importance. In the *Decretum,* Gratian gave his doctrine on dispensations in the canons themselves; he was not as reticent as was Ives who dared to speak of relaxations from the law only in the Prologue of his *Decretum,* as if fearing to speak of the law and a relaxation from it in the same breath.

In his *Decretum* (c. 1140), Gratian did not propose a new doctrine on dispensations; he rather promoted the doctrine of some of his predecessors, principally Bernaldus, Ives and Alger. His definition of a dispensation coincides with the one advanced by these authors. Gratian stated that a dispensation was a "relaxation of the severity of the law stemming out of mercy,"[1] or a "curtailing and relaxation of canonical precepts for the benefit and the necessity of the Church."[2] At times he even approached the concept of a dispensation in the strict sense of the term as accepted today, for he stated that the severity of the canons may at times be relaxed in behalf of a person.[3]

### Article 1. In the *Decretum Gratiani*

### *Section A. Author*

Gratian, following the doctrine set down by Bernaldus, vindicated the right of the Roman Pontiff to grant dispensations

[1] "Nisi rigor disciplinae quandoque relaxetur ex dispensatione misericordiae." — *Dictum Gratiani,* c. 5, C. I., q. 7.

[2] "Aliquando enim pro necessitate vel ecclesiae utilitate mutilantur et relaxantur praecepta canonica." — *Dictum Gratiani,* c. 23, C. I, q. 7.

[3] Cf. *Dictum Gratiani,* post c. 10, C. I, q. 7.

from the general laws of the Church. The fundamental reason for the papal prerogative in granting dispensations, according to Gratian, was the fact that the pope was the author and thus the lord over all laws.[4] Moreover, he stated that it was permissible for the pope to grant that which was prohibited by the general law.[5] This power of the popes was not contrary to the law because various councils made provisions in ecclesiastical law for just such papal action.[6] This cannot be construed as a vindication of the exclusive power of the pope to dispense, since it was not the intention of Gratian to attempt to solve this question in his *Dictum* after c. 16, C. XXV, q. 1. He rather gave a reply to those who alleged that the pope lacked jurisdiction to grant dispensations from the general laws of the Church.[7] It did, however, open the gates for the commentators to vindicate the exclusive right of the popes over general decrees of the Church.

Concerning the powers of the bishops to grant dispensations, Gratian did not explicitly deny them this right, nor did he speak of delegated powers that the bishops might have received from the popes. The bishops apparently granted various dispensations because Gratian spoke of Episcopal dispensations. He did, however, reserve certain dispensations to papal authority, as for example, the dispensation accorded to a person who entered a second marriage after the death of his first wife in order to permit him to receive the diaconate.[8]

[4] Cf. *Dictum Gratiani* ad c. 16, C. XXV, q. 1: "Nonnumquam vero seu iubendo, seu difiniendo, seu aliter agendo, se decretorum dominos et conditores esse ostendunt."

[5] "Licet itemque sibi [primae Sedi] contra generalia decreta, specialia privilegia indulgere, et speciali beneficio concedere quod generali prohibetur decreto." — *Loc. cit.*

[6] "Unde in nonnullis capitulis conciliorum, cum aliquid observandum decernitur, statim subinfertur: 'Nisi auctoritas Romanae Ecclesiae aliter impetraverit,' vel, 'salvo tamen in omnibus iure sanctae Romanae Ecclesiae,' vel, 'salva tamen in omnibus apostolica auctoritate.'" — *Dictum Gratiani* post c. 16, C. XXV, q. 1.

[7] Cf. Brys, *De Dispensatione in Iure Canonico,* p. 85.

[8] C. 7, D. XXXIV.

## *Section B. Causes*

The exclusive power of the popes to dispense from the general laws of the Church had not as yet been fully vindicated. Thus the effect which resulted from the lack of a cause when a bishop or other subordinate agent granted a dispensation from a general law was not discussed by Gratian. Whenever there was a discussion in the *Decretum* concerning a cause for a dispensation, it always concerned papal dispensations. Gratian demanded a reasonable cause before any dispensation could be granted. He indicated that only common necessity or benefit were acceptable causes.[9] He arrived at this conclusion despite the fact that in a previous canon he listed six canonical causes, some private in nature, which were deemed sufficient for a dispensation. These were: because of the times, in behalf of a person, in the interest of piety, necessity, benefit, and a consequence of an event.[10] Since some of these causes were of a private nature, the logical conclusion seems to be that these were considered in relation to the common benefit which would accrue at least indirectly to the Church in general from dispensations granted for these causes. Gratian, nevertheless, left the door open for the possibility of dispensations being granted for strictly private causes.

The validity or lawfulness of dispensations granted without a cause was still an abstruse question which Gratian did not consider as a possibility since he gave it no mention in his *Decretum*. He gave an indication, however, of the future concepts concerning subreption and obreption as voiding a rescript—and the same may be said for a dispensation—when he asserted that a rescript thus obtained was worthless.[11]

[9] Cf. *Dictum Gratiani* post c. 23, C. I, q. 7; c. 18, D. XXXIV; c. 68, D. L.; c. 1, D. LV.

[10] Cf. *Dictum Gratiani* ad c. 5, C. I, q. 7.

[11] Cf. c. 16, C. XXV, q. 2: "ea [illa sacra concessa] vero, quae subreptione, vel falsis precibus forsitan impetrantur, nullum supplicantibus ferre remedium."

## Article 2. In the Decretists

During the time preceding Rufinus, the word *dispensation* was accepted in the broader sense of the word, that is, exemptions, mutations, and even abrogations of the law. With the new strict juridical notion as given by Rufinus (1165), namely, that dispensation is a derogation of the severity of the law for a just cause in a given case by one in authority,[12] a more definite teaching on dispensations evolved. Most of the authors who came after the time of Rufinus accepted his concept of a dispensation.

### *Section A. Author*

The Decretists followed almost exclusively the teaching of Gratian concerning the power of the pope to grant dispensations. They vindicated the power of the pope to dispense from the general laws of the Church on the grounds that being the author of the law, he could allow exceptions to the law.[13] From this vindication of exclusive papal power by the early Decretists and Decretalists, it would seem that the bishops were considered as subordinates whenever they granted dispensations from papal decrees or any other general legislation of the Church. The Decretists, however, did not define very clearly the power of the bishops nor of any other subordinate, for that matter. Some denied the bishops any power whatsoever; others conceded that the bishops could grant dispensations but were to be considered as subordinates to the pope.[14] The bishops were considered as capable agents to grant dispensations whenever such power was granted them by the canons: this faculty was delegated either by law or by the popes.[15]

[12] "Est itaque dispensatio justa causa faciente ab eo, cujus interest, canonici rigoris facta derogatio."—*Die Summa Decretorum des Magister Rufinus* (ed. H. Singer, Paderborn, 1902), c. 6, C. I, q. 7, p. 234.

[13] Cf. Brys, *De Dispensatione in Iure Canonico,* p. 138.

[14] Cf. *ibid.,* p. 143.

[15] Cf. Huggucio, Mss. cited by Brys, *De Dispensatione in Iure Canonico,* p. 144, footnote 4.

### *Section B. Causes*

Now that Rufinus had given a strict juridical concept of a dispensation, a private cause was admitted as a legitimate one for which a dispensation could be granted. Necessity and benefit were still the major causes, but even if they were in relation to a private good, they were considered as sufficient. The Decretists, however, did not question further the validity of a dispensation when a just and reasonable cause was lacking. Hugguccio (post 1185) admitted the validity of a dispensation when granted by the legislator without a just cause, but considered such a dispensation to be illicit.[16] Nothing as yet had been set down at this time concerning the validity of a dispensation granted by a subordinate when a just cause was not present. If the teaching of Hugguccio is accepted, however, such a dispensation would, *a fortiori*, be illicit.

## Article 3. In the Decretals and Decretalists

The fundamental difference between the Decretists and the Decretalists in the manner in which the subject of a dispensation was considered, is found in the fact that the Decretists aimed at defining it, inquiring into its causes, objects and effects, whereas the Decretalists rather interpreted the texts of the law and attempted to propose practical rules about the valid and licit use of dispensations. The Decretalists accepted the strict notion of a dispensation, following the *glossa ordinaria* of the *Decretum*,[17] and evolved the doctrine concerning the required causes for a dispensation. They discussed the causes which were required for valid and licit dispensations when granted by the legislator, and also by those who had delegated powers.[18]

From the time of the Decretals of Gregory IX (1234), those who were not authors of a law, had to be considered as subordinates when granting a dispensation; the power of

[16] Cf. Mss. cited by Brys, *op. cit.*, p. 119, footnote 3.

[17] "dispensatio est iuris communis relaxatio facta cum causae cognitione ab eo qui ius habet dispensandi." — *Glossa* ad verbum *plerisque*, c. 5, C. I, q. 7.

[18] Cf. Brys, *De Dispensatione in Iure Canonico*, p. 161.

the bishops was limited to specific instances permitted them by law.[19] The Decretalists began to distinguish between causes which were deemed necessary before a legislator could dispense from his own laws, and the causes which had to be present before a subordinate dispensing agent could grant valid dispensations.

### *Section A. Causes*

It can be said that the Decretalists followed the doctrine proposed by Gratian and the Decretists concerning the causes for a dispensation. They accepted the teaching that a dispensation could be granted for such reasons as circumstances of the times, in behalf of a person, in the interest of piety, for necessity or benefit, or as a consequence of an event. The insistence upon common necessity or benefit of the Church in general was rapidly becoming obsolete, and causes of a strictly private nature were accepted as sufficient reasons for which dispensations could be granted. Such causes as intellectual knowledge, good morality, dignity, and old age were advanced as acceptable sufficient reasons.[20]

The Decretals of Gregory IX, however, still preserved the causes of common necessity and benefit for certain types of dispensations.[21]

The Decretalists who commented upon the Decretals of Gregory IX, although agreeing unanimously that a cause had to be present before a dispensation could be granted, disagreed as to the nature of the required cause. They all agreed, however, that the cause had to be a just one.[22] Some demanded

[19] Cf. Innocentius IV, *Commentaria in Quinque Libros Decretalium* (Venetiis, 1570), c. 6, X, *de Constitutionibus,* I, 2.

[20] Cf. Innocent III in a decretal to Hubert Walter, Archbishop of Canterbury (1200), in c. 20, X, *de electione et electi potestate,* I, 6.

[21] Cf. c. 19, X, *de sententia et re iudicata,* II, 27; c. 2, X, *de desponsatione impuberum,* IV, 2, where an "urgentissima necessitas interveniens" is demanded; c. 8, X, *de aetate et qualitate et ordine praeficiendorum,* I, 14.

[22] Cf. Raymund of Pennafort, *Summa de Poenitentia et Matrimonio* (Veronae, 1744), Lib. III, tit. 29, § 2, *de dispensationibus,* p. 345; Innocentius IV, *Commentaria in Quinque Libros Decretalium,* c. 6, X, *de statu monachorum,* III, 35; Hostiensis, *Commentaria in Quinque Decretalium Libros* (5 vols. in 3, Venetiis, 1581), c. 19, 54, X, *de electione,* I, 6.

also that the cause be certain, before a dispensation could be granted.[23] In the Decretals of Boniface VIII (1298), a reasonable cause was mentioned as necessary for a dispensation whenever a bishop granted dispensations.[24] Guido de Baysio (†1313) contended that it was prohibited to grant a dispensation unless a just and certain cause was present.[25]

### *Section B. Effect of lack of a cause*

The Decretalists added a new phase to their treatises on dispensations. They proposed the question of lawfulness and validity of a dispensation when a proper cause for the relaxation of the law was either lacking or the reason advanced was false. Huggucio was the first to consider the question but he dealt only with papal dispensations, and concluded that the pope could validly dispense even without a just cause since he was the author of the law.[26] The Decretalists, however, delved further into the question. They examined the effect of a dispensation from the general law when granted without a just cause by an agent who was subordinate to the pope. The accepted principle was that whenever any subordinate granted a dispensation from the law of his superior, the dispensation was both illicit and invalid if a just cause was lacking. Raymond of Pennafort, moreover, held that a bishop who dared to grant dispensations without a just cause was to be punished, even deposed, if he were accused of this infraction.[27]

[23] Cf. Durandus, *Speculum Iuris* (4 vols. in 3, Venetiis: apud Juntas, 1577), Lib. I, partic. 1, Rubrica *de Dispensatione,* § 9; Hostiensis, *Summa Aurea* (Venetiis, 1570), Lib. V, tit. *de Remissionibus,* Rubrica *de Dispensationibus,* § 1.

[24] C. 14, X, *de electione,* I, 6, in VI°: "prout causa rationabilis id exposcit."

[25] Cf. *Commentarium super Sexto Decretalium* (Venetiis, 1577), c. 14, I. 6.

[26] Cf. Mss. fol. 564, cited by Brys, *De Dispensatione in Iure Canonico,* p. 119, footnote 3.

[27] "Episcopus qui sine justa causa dispenset puniendus est, et propter indiscretam dispensationem poena depositionis infligenda, si de hoc fuerit accusatus." —*Summa de Poenitentia et Matrimonio,* Lib. III, tit. XXIX, § 2, *de Dispensationibus.*

Innocent IV (1243-1254) went even farther by declaring that a dispensation granted by a subordinate was invalid if no investigation was made into the causes advanced in the petition. He explained the difference between the position of the legislator in relation to his own laws, and that of the delegate granting a dispensation from the law of his superior.[28] Hostiensis also proposed a similar doctrine, namely, that although the pope could dispense validly without a cause, others, i.e., subordinates, could not grant dispensations without a cause, and if they dared to do so, the dispensation was invalid.[29]

Abbas Panormitanus (1386-1453) explained that the word *dispensation* implied that whenever the power to grant dispensations was delegated to a subordinate, this power could be used only when a reason was present; otherwise the dispensation was invalid.[30] This was true whenever a subordinate granted dispensations without a reasonable cause, and such action was to be punished, since it was rather a dissipation than a dispensation.[31]

In the era immediately preceding the Council of Trent, Felinus Sandeus (†1503) repeated the very same doctrine, contending that the power delegated to a subordinate was not of the same intensity as that of the legislator. In order that a subordinate might grant dispensations validly, a reasonable cause had to be present.[32]

28 "Item licet conditori constitutionis dispensare ex certa scientia contra suam constitutionem, non tamen aliis, quibus concessum est dispensare, licet dispensare nisi cum causae cognitione, et si dispensant non valet dispensatio, vel revocatur et ipsi peccant et puniuntur."—*Commentaria in Quinque Libros Decretalium,* c. 6, X, *de statu monachorum,* III, 35; cf. also *op. cit.,* c. 15, X, *de temporibus ordinationis,* I, 4.

29 "Alii tamen quam Papae contra iura sine causa dispensare non licet, quod si praesumpserit, non valet dispensatio, vel revocatur et ipse punitur." —*Commentaria in Quinque Decretalium Libros,* c. 6, X, *de statu monachorum,* III, 35, n. 29.

30 Cf. *Commentaria in Quinque Libros Decretalium,* super c. 6, X, *de statu monachorum,* III, 35, n. 17.

31 Cf. *op. cit.,* super c. 54, X, *de electione,* I, 6, n. 38.

32 *Commentaria in Quinque Libros Decretalium* (2 vols., Venetiis, 1570), Lib. I, tit. III, c. 31, col. 796.

## *Section C. Effect of subreption and obreption*

Not only did the Decretalists explore the causes required for a valid grant of a dispensation and the effect that a lack of a cause would have, but they also examined cases wherein subreption and obreption was practiced. The Gregorian Decretals advanced the possibility of obreption in a petition for a dispensation; and a dispensation given in a particular case was declared invalid, since it was fraudulently obtained from the pope.[33] *A fortiori,* it can be concluded that the same would obtain, had the dispensation been granted by a subordinate agent. Hostiensis followed the doctrine of the Decretals that a dispensation was rendered invalid by the expression of a falsehood or by suppression of the truth, if the dispensation would have been denied had the truth been known.[34]

Abbas Panormitanus in his various treaties gave a closer scrutiny to the question of subreption, and in each instance arrived at the same conclusion: a dispensation is *ipso iure* invalid when subreption was practiced. One could determine the validity of a favor, not by examining the guilt of the petitioner, but rather by examining the intention of the author of the dispensation. If the dispensing agent had known the truth, he would not so readily have granted the favor by which a statute was set aside.[35] It is quite clear that the Decretalists considered subreption and obreption as vitiating a dispensation whether it was granted by the pope or by a subordinate dispensing authority.

[33] Cf. c. 6, X, *de consanguinitate et affinitate,* IV, 14; the same principle is repeated in c. 2, X, *de filiis presbyterorum,* I, 11, in V°.

[34] *Commentaria in Quinque Decretalium Libros,* c. 54, X, *de electione,* I, 6: "Sic igitur dispensatio propter expressionem falsitatis vel suppressionem veritatis redditur invalida. Quod intelligas esse verum, ubi falsitas exprimitur vel tacetur veritas de his quae circa dispensationem obtinendam consistunt, quibus tacitis vel expressis fuisset dispensatio denegata, qualia sunt illa quae hic tanguntur." Cf. also, *op. cit.,* c. 6, X, *de consanguinitate et affinitate,* IV, 6.

[35] Cf. *Commentarium* super c. 54, X, *de electione,* I, 6, n. 13; super c. 19, *de Rescriptis,* I; super c. 6, *de consanguinitate et affinitate,* IV, 6, n. 5; Consilium 38, pars II, c. *In quaestione,* n. 1.

# CHAPTER V

# DISPENSATIONS FROM THE COUNCIL OF TRENT TILL THE CODE

## Article 1. Decrees of the Council of Trent

The Council of Trent, convoked by Pope Paul III, on May 22, 1542, held its first session on December 13, 1545. The Bull of Confirmation of the General Council of Trent was given by Pope Pius IV on January 26, 1564. During the intervening years, twenty-five sessions were held, none of which was exclusively devoted to formulating rules and regulations which would serve as general norms for granting dispensations. The Fathers did, however, during their deliberations in the various sessions, consider it advisable at times to repeat the generally accepted norms, and to enact new ones where they deemed it necessary. They reiterated the accepted concept of dispensation, by stating that "it is at times expedient to relax the bond of the law in order that cases and necessities which arise may be more fully met for the common good."[1]

### *Section A. Causes*

The Council of Trent set down the obligation that its decrees and canons were to be observed by all; the Fathers, nevertheless, mitigated their own stringent ruling by permitting dispensations in particular cases under certain conditions. An urgent and just reason, or a greater good, were the acceptable causes for a dispensation. The *greater good* was not explained further whether it was to be a public good or whether a private good sufficed; nor was it stated that a public cause was necessary before a dispensation could be granted. A further condition imposed by the Fathers stipulated that the matter was to be investigated and only after mature deliberation could a dispensation be permitted.[2] The one explicit

[1] "Expedit legis vinculum relaxare, ut plenius evenientibus casibus et necessitatibus pro communi utilitate satisfiat." — Sess. XXV, *de ref.*, c. 18.

[2] Cf. Sess. XXV, *de ref.*, c. 18.

instance where a public cause was specified by the Council as being requisite, concerned the dispensation from the impediment of affinity in the second degree.[3] A *true and reasonable* cause which had to be legally proven before the ordinary, was demanded by the holy Council for a dispensation from personal residence while in possession of a benefice requiring such a residence.[4] Beyond these few instances, the Council of Trent did not give any detailed enumeration of causes prescribed by law for any particular dispensation.

### *Section B. Powers granted to bishops*

Within the various decrees of the Council of Trent, can be found instances wherein bishops were granted faculties to act as delegates of the Holy See, in other words, they were granted delegated faculties to act in the name of the Holy See. These faculties usually were not concerned with the power to grant dispensations, but rather with supervision of ecclesiastical matters in the name of the Holy Father.[5] The particular case wherein a bishop was delegated by the Council to act in the name of the Holy See relative to a dispensation, had for its object favors granted *in forma gratiosa* by the Roman Curia. Such dispensations do not take effect until the ordinary, as a delegate of the Holy See, has established extra-judicially and in a summary manner, that the petition is free of subreption and obreption.[6]

In certain cases, the Council deemed it fitting explicitly to extend to the ordinaries powers of dispensation, while at the same time allowing some matters to be decided by the prudent judgment of the bishop. Whether these faculties are to be

[3] "In secundo gradu [affinitatis] nunquam dispensetur nisi . . ob publicam causam." — Sess. XXIV, *de ref. matrim.*, c. 5.

[4] Cf. Sess. VI, *de ref.*, c. 2.

[5] Cf. Sess. V, *de ref.*, c. 1, 2; Sess. VI, *de ref.*, c. 3; Sess. VII, *de ref.*, c. 6; Sess. XIII, *de ref.*, c. 5; Sess. XIV, *de ref.*, c. 4; Sess. XXI, *de ref.*, c. 3, 5, 6, 7, 8; Sess. XXII, *Decretum de observantia et vitandis in celebratione missae;* Sess. XXII, *de ref.*, c. 3, 5, 6, 8, 10; Sess. XXIV, *de ref.*, c. 9, 10, 11, 14; Sess. XXV, *de regularibus*, c. 8, 9.

[6] Cf. Sess. XXII, *de ref.*, c. 5.

considered as delegated by law, or as ordinary powers of the bishops remains as a disputed question. It would seem, however, that these powers were vested by law in the office of the Episcopacy, and thus were vicarious ordinary powers. The instance wherein the decrees of the Council of Trent communicated such powers to the bishops are few in number, so it would perhaps be useful to examine each individually.

1. The ordination of a cleric who did not possess a benefice was forbidden by the Council; clerics who possessed a patrimony or a pension could not be ordained unless the bishop had decided that their ordination was beneficial or necessary for the Church. The bishop was obliged, however, to investigate each and every case in order to ascertain that the patrimony really existed and was sufficient for the cleric's sustenance.[7] It is quite apparent that the faculty to dispense was herein conceded to the bishop.

2. While reaffirming the age-old discipline of the Church in regard to the interstices which must be observed between the different Orders, the Council nonetheless, conceded the bishops the faculty to dispense from the obligation to observe the spacing of time between Orders as specified by law, whenever the bishops deemed it expedient, or whenever need or necessity of the Church warranted such action. This faculty was conceded for the minor orders as well as for the subdiaconate,[8] the diaconate,[9] and those promoted to the priesthood; these last could also be granted a dispensation from the obligation of celebrating Mass on the prescribed days. This dispensation could have been granted only when a legitimate reason was present and provided that they were promoted to the priesthood from the subdiaconate, by-passing the diaconate, and had not exercised the ministry.[10]

[7] Cf. Sess. XXI, *de ref.*, c. 2.

[8] Cf. Sess. XXIII, *de ref.*, c. 11.

[9] Cf. Sess. XXIII, *de ref.*, c. 13.

[10] "Ad presbyteratus ordinem assumuntur . . . qui non modo in diaconatu ad minus annum integrum, nisi ob ecclesiae utilitatem ac necessitatem aliud episcopo videatur, ministraverint, . . . Cum promotis per saltum, si non ministraverint, episcopus ex legitima causa possit dispensare de missae celebratione." — Sess. XXIII, *de ref.*, c. 14.

3. The publication of three banns before a marriage was prescribed, but the Fathers foresaw that there could be cases wherein the publications would cause a marriage to be maliciously hindered. In such cases only one publication had to be made before the marriage was celebrated, and the other two before its consummation. This would give time to discover whether or not any impediment to the marriage existed. The Council, moreover, granted the faculty to dispense from all three publications should the ordinary find it advisable to do so. It was left to the prudence and judgment of the bishop to determine when such a dispensation was needed.[11]

4. The bishops were authorized by the Council to dispense those who contracted an irregularity and a suspension by committing a secret crime. They could not, however, dispense those who were guilty of wilful homicide, or if the crime had already been brought to trial.[12] They were also granted powers to dispense from public penances which were imposed for a public crime. The public penance was commuted to a private penance if in the bishop's judgment it was expedient to do so.[13]

5. When a vacancy in a parochial church occurred, and the office entailed the *cura animarum,* definite rules had to be followed by the bishop in making the appointment to fill the vacancy. The Council prescribed a public examination before three synodal examiners for all of the candidates. This examination delved into their age, morals, learning, and prudence. Under certain conditions, enumerated by the Holy Council,—namely, if the financial burden of the examination could not be sustained by the parochial church in question, if no candidates had presented themselves, or if there was a danger of violent quarrels and disturbances due to factions and dissensions,—the ordinary could dispense with this formality and permit a private examination if he consci-

[11] Cf. Sess. XXIV, *de ref. matrim.,* c. 1.

[12] Cf. Sess. XXIV, *de ref.,* c. 6.

[13] Cf. Sess. XXIV, *de ref.,* c. 8.

entiously and with the advice of the examiners deemed this to be the best course of action.[14]

6. The Holy Council reaffirmed that the cloister of nuns must be observed and imposed strict penalties for any violation or disobedience. No nun after her profession was allowed to go out of the monastery under any pretext whatever, not even for a brief time. The faculty to dispense from this regulation was granted to the bishops, providing there was a legitimate reason why a cloistered nun would find it necessary to leave the monastery temporarily.[15] Not only was the cloister to be observed by those within, but also no outsider was permitted to enter the cloister of a monastery. This law, too, was subject to a dispensation either by a bishop or the superior in necessary cases only.[16]

### *Section C. Effect of lack of a Cause*

The Fathers of the Council of Trent made no specific mention of what effect a lack of a cause would have upon a given dispensation. In two instances, however, they declared that if there was deception in the petition for a dispensation, the dispensation was ineffectual. 1) When the Roman Curia granted a dispensation in *forma gratiosa,* it became the duty of the bishop to examine the truthfulness of the petition. If the bishop should have discovered that either obreption or subreption had been present, the dispensation was vitiated and was considered as having no effect.[17] 2) The Fathers imposed the obligation that all the sacred canons were to be observed accurately. If, however, a case should have been present wherein an urgent and just cause, and at times a greater good indicated a dispensation, it was to be granted, but only after a most mature deliberation, and gratis; any dispensation granted otherwise would have to be regarded as surreptitious.[18] The Fathers thus showed their intention

[14] Cf. Sess. XXIV, *de ref.*, c. 18.
[15] Cf. Sess. XXV, *de regularibus,* c. 5.
[16] Cf. Sess. XXV, *de regularibus,* c. 5.
[17] Cf. Sess. XXII, *de ref.*, c. 5.
[18] Cf. Sess. XXV, *de ref.*, c. 18.

that a dispensation was not to be granted at random, but that a definite and true cause had to be present for validity.

## Article 2. Post-Tridentine Doctrine

### *Section A. Legislation*

After the Council of Trent, there was little legislation concerning the causes necessary for a dispensation since the decrees of the Council were in force and no new legislation was imperative. There were, however, from time to time reiterations of the unanimously accepted norms. Thus, for example, Pope Benedict XIV in his Constitution, *Ad Apostolicae* (Feb. 25, 1742), reaffirmed that it was the duty of the Holy See to watch diligently so that dispensations were not granted except for serious reasons. Furthermore, those who petitioned for a dispensation were required to express a cause, since the validity of the dispensation was dependent upon the assertion and the verification of the cause. Should there have been no cause, the dispensation was considered null and void.[19] The Sacred Congregation for the Propagation of the Faith also reminded the bishops by its decree that they were not to grant dispensations unless an urgent and just reason warranted such action, or some greater benefit required it. Even when these conditions existed, the decrees of the Council of Trent still obtained and had to be observed.[20]

[19] "Ad Apostolicae servitutis Nostrae ministerium pertinet sedula invigilare cura, ut dispensationes super gradibus affinitatis, seu consanguinitatis, intra quos matrimonia contrahi prohibentur, vel super aliis a Sacris Canonibus statutis impedimentis, nisi ex debitis causis non concedantur. . . .Sane quidem ad dispensationes obtinendas ab iis qui eas postulant, in supplici libello causae pro illis consequendis exprimi solent; . . . cum expressio causarum, earumque verificatio, ad substantiam et validitatem dispensationis pertineat, illisque deficientibus, gratia nulla, ac irrita sit, nullamque executionem mereatur."—*Codicis Iuris Canonici Fontes,* cura Emi Petri Card. Gasparri editi (9 vols., Romae: Typis Polyglottis Vaticanis, 1923-1939. Vols. VII-IX, ed. cura et studio Emi Iustiniani Card. Serédi), n. 325. (hereafter cited as *Fontes*).

[20] Decretum, 13 apr. 1807, n. IX: "Sedulo etiam caveant tam Administrator patriarchalis, quam reliqui Episcopi, ne dispensationes largiantur, nisi urgens et iusta ratio, et maior quandoque utilitas id postulet; ideoque nunquam dispensent, nisi causa cognita, ac summa maturitate, atque gratis, iuxta

### *Section B. Practice of the Roman Curia*

The formation of the jurisprudence concerning the validity of dispensations can be gathered from the mode of action of the various Sacred Congregations, which appeared in their Instructions and in their replies to questions proposed by the bishops. When the bishops of Ireland were granted extraordinary faculties, for example, to dispense in the second and third degree of relationship, three conditions were imposed, one of which stipulated that there be an urgent need for such dispensations. The urgent need was also interpreted so as to include a real and very important benefit, which was deemed as sufficient cause for which a dispensation could be granted. If any of the three conditions, namely, that the recipient be a subject of the dispensing authority, the necessity be urgent, and the dispensation be granted *gratis,* were lacking, the dispensation was invalid.[21]

In an Instruction of the Sacred Congregation for the Propagation of the Faith, the necessity of a legitimate and grave cause for dispensations from matrimonial impediments was prescribed. This cause necessarily had to be in proportion to the gravity of the law from which the dispensation was granted. The Instruction moreover, deplored the omission of the essentials which needed to be expressed in the petition for a dispensation, lest the dispensation be vitiated. It further stipulated that everyone had to abide by the above mentioned norms not only in petitions for dispensations from the Holy See but also when the petitions were addressed to one who had delegated powers to dispense, otherwise these delegated faculties suffered abuse.[22] If obreption or subreption was perpetrated in the petition for a dispensation in such a way that the sole final cause proposed was surrepti-

mandatum Sacri Concilii Tridentini.—*Collectanea S. Congregationis de Propaganda Fide* (2 vols., Romae: Typographia Polyglottis S. C. de Prop. Fide, 1907), n. 692 (hereafter cited as *Collectanea S. C. de Prop. Fide*).

[21] Cf. S. C. de Prop. Fide, 17 febr. 1772—*Collectanea S. C. de Prop. Fide,* n. 486; *Fontes,* n. 4554.

[22] Cf. Instr., 9 maii 1877 — *Collectanea S. C. de Prop. Fide,* n. 1470; *Fontes,* n. 4890.

tious, the dispensation was invalid and could not be executed by the Apostolic Delegate.[23]

The jurisprudence concerning dispensations granted without a cause, or for unjust or falsified causes, can perhaps best be gleaned from the practice of the Roman Rota in cases alleging nullity of marriage on the grounds of invalid dispensations. The particular decision in a given case need not be considered; it suffices to study the principles as enunciated by the Rota in each such case. Amongst the earliest decisions published by the Sacred Rota in its *Decisiones,* the question of a possible invalid dispensation was proposed on the basis that no causes were mentioned in the rescript granting the dispensation from the impediment of disparity of cult. Although the contention was not verified in fact, the Rota set down the principles by which it was guided while determining the validity of the dispensation. The major premise quoted Cardinal Gasparri, stating that a delegate cannot dispense validly except for a cause which was accepted by the practice of the Holy See as a final cause; nor could a cause which is considered as merely impulsive by the Roman Curia, be considered as efficacious in granting a valid dispensation. Furthermore, when faculties were granted to a bishop as a delegate, he was admonished that they were to be used only when a just and grave cause warranted its use.[24] Should there have

[23] *S. C. C., S. Claudii,* 24 aug. 1907: "Imo obreptio vel subreptio in themate versatur circa causam finalem concessionis; hinc si praeter falso adductam causam finalem, aliae finales et sufficientes non extent, dispensatio vitiatur; ideoque dispensationes, hac causa reticita obtentae, per se nullae sunt et a Delegato Apostolico non possunt executioni demandari seu fulminari."—*Fontes,* n. 4342.

[24] S.R.R., *Nullitas matrimonii,* 30 iunii 1910, Decisio XXIII, coram R.P.D. Michaeli Lega, Decano, n. 10: "Sane docet Card. Gasparri, *De Matrimonio,* n. 423: 'Delegatus nequit valide dispensare, nisi propter causam canonicam quae in praxi S. Sedis motiva est, et habere debet tamquam impulsivam tantum, vel prorsus inefficacem eam causam quae talis est in praxi Romanae Curiae; secus non solum illicite sed et invalide dispensat'. Nec minus clara est praescriptio quae continetur in tenore facultatum delegatarum quae ita concluduntur: 'Voluit tamen Sanctitas Sua, et omnino praecipit ut praedictus Episcopus superioribus facultatibus, justis dumtaxat gravibusque accedentibus

been a doubt whether the cause proposed was a just one, the dispensation was valid, nor did it lose its validity if it was later proven that the cause was of lesser value than when first appraised: this was verified even if the dispensation was granted by a delegate.[25]

In order to inspect the history of the jurisprudence in similar cases it may be well to include the practice of the Roman Rota in its decisions even after the promulgation of the Code of Canon Law. In a 1926 case, (coram Florczak) some very pertinent observations were made concerning the need of a just and reasonable cause for a dispensation granted by a subordinate, otherwise the dispensation would have been invalid because of lack of jurisdiction. If obreption, whether perpetrated fraudulently or in good faith, was practiced by alleging a cause which was false and without which the dispensation would not have been granted, the dispensation was null *ipso iure*. The subordinate dispensing agent, moreover, had to adapt himself to the regulations of the Roman Curia when he was in the process of determining whether the proferred cause was just and reasonable in any given petition for a dispensation from a matrimonial impediment.[26]

A further question was proposed: what is the effect of the false judgment of the dispensing agent concerning the exist-

causis, uteretur'." — *Sacrae Romanae Rotae Decisiones seu Sententiae, quae prodierunt anno 1909* — (Romae Typis Polyglottis Vaticanis, 1912 —), II (1910), 228-229 (hereafter cited *S.R.R. Decisiones*).

25 *Ibid.*, n. 11: "Et in dubio an concessa fuerit ex iusta causa, stat; nec revocatur si postea haec minus iusta apparuerit. . . . Quae valent etsi agatur de delegato aut de executore dispensationis." — *S.R.R. Decisiones*, II (1910), 229.

26 S.R.R., *Nullitas matrimonii*, 6 maii 1926, Decisio XXI, coram R.P.D. Josepho Florczak, n. 2: "Hinc, in casu obreptionis, sive ex dolo sive ex bona fide, si in instantia falso expressa est causa, sine qua superior non fuisset gratiam concessurus, haec est nulla ipso iure (this is quoted by the Rota from Gasparri, *De Matrimonio*, I, n. 381, nota 1). Ut vero inferior dispensans in impedimentis matrimonialibus iuris ecclesiastici recte existimet quae in casu est causa iusta et rationabilis, sequi debet easdem illas regulas, quae in iisdem casibus servantur in Curia Romana; nam vero delegatus legibus delegantis tenetur." — *S.R.R. Decisiones*, XVIII (1926), 167.

ence or the sufficiency of the final cause? If the error of the dispensing agent concerned the sufficiency of the alleged final cause, and even if it is later proven with certitude that the cause, although existing in fact, was not sufficient for this particular dispensation, the dispensation was nevertheless considered valid. This was in opposition to Diana who would extend this interpretation also to cases of error concerning the existence of the final cause, so that even if the alleged cause did not exist in fact, the dispensation would be valid. If on the other hand, it was proven with certitude that the dispensing agent erred concerning the existence of the cause the dispensation was invalid; but if there was a doubt concerning the existence of the cause, the act of dispensation was valid since in doubts, the validity of an act is upheld.[27]

The practice of the Roman Rota further demonstrates that when the alleged final cause for a dispensation was proven to be false and non-existent in fact, the dispensation was invalid. In a case wherein the only final cause proposed in the petition for a dispensation from the impediment of consanguinity in the second degree of the collateral line, was proven to be false, the Rota declared the marriage null due to an invalid dispensation. This decision was handed down in 1934 (coram

[27] *Ibid.*, n. 3: " quaeri solet, quaenam sint sequelae falsi iudicii quod superior sibi informet sive circa existentiam, sive circa sufficientiam causae motivae. In qua quaestione plura distinguenda sunt: equidem si orator falsum, etsi bona fide, exposuerit circa causam finalem in substantialibus, obreptio haec, ut iam vidimus, irritat dispensationem (praescindendo scilicet a nova canonis 1054 dispositione). Si vero error sit solius superioris rem minus recte existimantis, communiter traditur rem utrimque controverti: inspicienti penitus allatos textus, obvia conclusio videtur in casu merae *non existentiae causae* solum fortasse Diana explicite asserere validitatem dispensationis, quam alii — non exclusis Salmanticensibus, qui eius verba allegant — restringere videntur ad casum *merae sufficientiae,* definientes nimirum communiter, valere dispensationem si a Superiore falso aestimata sit sufficiens causa, quae postea *certo* constet, exstitisse quidem, sed non fuisse sufficientem. . Et ratio distinctionis obvia est consideranti, in casu non existentiae adhuc possidere legem, in casu non sufficientiae adhuc possidere facultatem. Haec. inquam, si postea certo constet errasse dispensatorem; nam si dubia res manet, pacificum est in dubio standum pro valore actus, etiamsi dubium vertatur circa existentiam causae." *S.R.R. Decisiones,* XVIII (1926), 169.

Wynen) when *nimia familiaritas* was alleged as the cause for the dispensation, whereas it was proven from the testimony of the plaintiff, the defendant and other witnesses, that the alleged cause was not verified in fact.[28]

### *Section C. Doctrine of the authors*

#### a. Power of the bishops to grant dispensations

The post-Tridentine authors followed the doctrine of the Decretalists and the legislation of the Council of Trent in their treatises on dispensation. The exception to this, however, concerned the power of the bishops to dispense in cases where the law did not explicitly prohibit a dispensation. The common opinion existing prior to the Council of Trent conceded such powers to the bishops.[29] A strong proponent of the opposite doctrine was the Abbas Panormitanus whose contention was that the bishop could dispense only in those cases which were permitted him by law.[30] Suarez (1548-1617) took up the opinion of the Abbas, reasoning that when the superior legislator proposed a law, he withdrew it from the power of any subordinate. It was not necessary for the superior explicitly to restrict the subordinate's power over such laws.[31] This opinion gained in favor so that within a relatively short time it became the commonly accepted doctrine amongst the authors.[32] Reiffenstuel (1642-1703) undertook a rather lengthy discussion on this question, adhering to the doctrine of Suarez. The bishops, or other subordinates could not ordi-

[28] Cf. S.R.R. *Nullitas matrimonii,* 16 iunii 1934, Decisio XLV, coram R.P.D. Arcturo Wynen — *S.R.R. Decisiones,* XXVI (1934), 393-407.

[29] Cf. *Glossa* ad c. 4, X, *de iudiciis,* II, 1.

[30] Cf. *Commentaria* ad c. 15, X, *de temporibus ordinationum et qualitate ordinandorum,* I, 11.

[31] *De Legibus,* Lib. VI, c. 14, nn. 4 - 6. — *Opera Omnia,* Vol. VI, pp. 67 - 68.

[32] Reiffenstuel, *Jus Canonicum Universum,* (Parisiis, 1864-1870) Lib. I, tit. 2, § 18, n. 465: dispensatio autem in Sacris Canonibus intelligitur prohibita nisi ubi eis [i.e. Episcopis] reperitur concessa vel expresse vel saltem tacite; cf. also St. Alphonsus, *Theologia Moralis* (ed. nova, 4 vols., Romae, 1905-1912) Lib. I, tract. 2, c. 4, n. 191; Benedictus XIV, *De Synodo Dioecesana* (Parmae, 1746), Lib. IX, c. 1, n. 6.

narily dispense from the Sacred Canons, from the Apostolic constitutions, or from the decrees of the General Councils, because the bishop as a subordinate did not possess any jurisdiction over the pope, or the General Councils, and furthermore the bishops as custodians of the law needed to observe it perfectly.[33]

The bishop could also dispense from the general laws of the Church in cases of urgent necessity when there was danger in delay and recourse to the Holy See was difficult. In such cases the bishop acted on the presumed faculty to grant dispensations since the Episcopal office required such faculties; otherwise the souls entrusted to his care would suffer great hardships in cases of urgent need. The presumption was that the faculty to dispense was granted by the pope in such instances.[34]

In cases which occurred rather frequently, such as dispensations from fast, and in cases of less important matters, the bishop could dispense from the general law of the Church. Reiffenstuel reiterated this commonly held doctrine. As his reasons he advanced the theory that although nothing was mentioned in law concerning such cases, nevertheless, one could reasonably presume that the pope would not insist that cases of daily occurrence should be referred to him; then, too, the Holy See could not be approached quickly enough in these matters which required immediate attention.[35]

### b. Effect of lack of a cause

From the time of the Decretalists, it has been the commonly accepted doctrine of the Church that a subordinate could not dispense lawfully or validly from the law of a

[33] Cf. *Jus Canonicum Universum,* Lib. I, tit. 2, § 18, n. 463.

[34] Cf. Reiffenstuel, ibid., n. 470; he followed the doctrine of Sanchez, *De Sancto Matrimonii Sacramento* (Venetiis, 1726), Lib. II, disp. 40, n. 3: "Quia, quamvis regulariter nequeat Episcopus in lege Pontificis aut Concilii dispensare, potest tamen in casu urgentis necessitatis, quando ad Pontificem aditus non patet"; and also Barbosa *Iuris Ecclesiastici Universi Libri Tres* (Lugduni, 1650), L. I, c. 11, § 6, n. 194.

[35] *Jus Canonicum Universum,* Lib. I, tit. 2, § 18, n. 472-473.

superior without a just and reasonable cause. The Council of Trent did not alter this accepted teaching, but rather approved and bolstered it.[36]

Suarez, writing shortly after the Council of Trent, gave reasons for this doctrine: a dispensation granted by a subordinate was unlawful and invalid because the *inferior* exceeded his powers. Power to dispense was granted to a subordinate by a Superior, with the condition that this faculty be used only for a just cause; should he have acted contrary to the will of the Superior, the *inferior* exceeded his mandate, thus rendering the dispensation null and void.[37] This doctrine was followed by other canonists of the seventeenth and eighteenth centuries.[38]

Not only was a just cause necessary, but an actual investigation of the cause was required for validity of a dispensation granted by a subordinate. The investigation was demanded to assure the reasonableness and justice of the alleged cause; the validity of the dispensation rested directly upon the investigation.[39] Sanchez went even farther by as-

[36] Cf. Sess. XXV, *de ref.*, c. 18.

[37] *De Legibus,* Lib. VI, c. 19, n. 1: "Nam de hac posteriori [dispensatione ab inferiore in lege superioris] omnes fatentur datam sine causa non solum esse illicitam, sed etiam esse invalidam, quia excedit potestatem dispensantis; non enim est efficax voluntas inferioris ad tollendum effectum per superiorem voluntatem constitutum, nisi quatenus ab ipso superiore concessum est: non autem verisimile esse concessum ut hoc possit inferiori sine causa. Et ideo tunc inferior excedit formam mandati et operatur sine potestate, et ideo actum nullum facit." — Opera Omnia, Vol. VI, p. 90; cf. also *De Voto,* Lib. VI, c. 17, n. 2-5 — Opera Omnia, Vol. XIV, pp. 1123-1124.

[38] Cf. Sanchez, *De Sancto Matrimoni Sacramento,* Lib. VIII, disp. 17, c. 4, wherein he asserted that no one contradicted this accepted doctrine; Barbosa, *Iuris Ecclesiastici Universi Libri Tres* (Lugduni, 1650), Lib. I, c. II, § 6, n. 198, and *De Officio et Potestate Episcopi* (3 vols., Lugduni, 1656), Pars II, alleg. 34, n. 1; De Justis, *Tractatus de Dispensationibus Matrimonialibus* (Venetiis, 1759) Lib. III, c. 1, n. 44; Reiffenstuel, *Jus Canonicum Universum,* Lib. I, tit. II, n. 483, and *Theologia Moralis* (7 ed., 2 vols., Mutinae, 1745) Tract. II, dist. 4, n. 21; Benedictus XIV, *De Synodo Dioecesana,* Lib. XIII, c. 5, n. 7.

[39] Suarez, *De Legibus,* Lib. VI, c. 19, n. 2: "Solum oportet advertere communiter jurisperitos docere necessarium esse, ad valorem dispensationis ab

serting that even if the cause was truly a legitimate one, but if the subordinate dispensing agent did not investigate it, the dispensation would be invalid, because the bounds of the mandate to dispense were overstepped.[40] The doctrine that it was essential for the validity of the dispensation to investigate the alleged cause, obtained until 1885 when the clause *si veritate niti reperis* was changed to *si vera sint exposita,* in the formula of concession of dispensations.[41]

Sanchez advanced the question of the validity of a dispensation when the alleged cause was found to be unjust, and concluded that such a dispensation by a subordinate dispensing agent would be invalid because an unjust cause is tantamount to no cause at all. He tempered this conclusion, however, in those cases wherein the subordinate prudently and in good faith adjudged the alleged cause as just and reasonable, even though later it was found to be insufficient.[42] Barbosa accepted this theory when he added that such a dispensation would also be lawful even though there should be a doubt as to the justice of the alleged cause, so long as the dispensing agent was in good faith and prudently judged that the cause was just.[43] An opponent of this theory is found in

inferiore datae ut dispenset causa cognita." — Opera Omnia, vol. VI, p. 90. Also cf. Barbosa, *De Officio et Potestate Episcopi,* Pars II, alleg. 33, n. 4; Reiffenstuel, *Jus Canonicum Universum,* Lib. I, tit. 2, § 18, n. 483, and *Appendix ad Quartum Librum,* § IV, n. 31.

[40] *De Sancto Matrimonii Sacramento,* Lib. VIII, disp. 17, n. 10: "Sed merito dubitabis quid dicendum de dispensatione facta ab inferiori in lege superioris, non praecognita causa, quando revera erat causa legitima: an valida sit? Pars negans suaderi videtur, quod dispensans excesserit suae commissionis limites. Nam censetur sibi facultas dispensandi commissa praemissa causae cognitione."

[41] Cf. Decisio S.C.S. Officii, 28 aug. 1885 apud Zitelli, *De Dispensationibus Matrimonialibus* (Romae, 1887) p. 94.

[42] *De Sancto Matrimonii Sacramento,* Lib. VIII, disp. 17, nn. 7-8: "Similiter non valet dispensatio inferioris in lege superioris, licet sit aliqualis causa, si tamen eam illegitimam esse constet. Quia idem est in hoc non esse causam, et non esse justam. . Hoc autem limitarem, nisi prudenter ac bona fide judicarit praelatus causam esse justam. Tunc enim credo valere dispensationem, licet vere non fuerit causa sufficiens."

[43] *Iuris Ecclesiastici Universi Libri Tres,* Lib. I, c. 11, § 6, n. 198: "Sufficit

Basil Pontius (†1629), who held that, even if the subordinate in good faith adjudged the cause to be just, the dispensation was nonetheless invalid.[44]

c. Effect of subreption and obreption

Another question developed by the authors concerned obreption, subreption and error in the petition for a dispensation. In their treatises they made the natural distinction between falsehood or error in the *causa motiva* and the *causa impulsiva*. There was unanimous agreement as to the definition of the motivating or final cause, namely that it moves the dispensing agent to act, and if it were not expressed, he would not be apt to use his dispensatory powers, or, if he did dispense, it would be conditionally and with limitation. The impulsive cause was defined as that which does not move the dispensing agent to act, but rather facilitates the granting of the dispensation, which could and most likely, would have been granted even if this cause was not mentioned.[45]

When the final cause was found to be objectively false, even if the obreption should have been caused through ignorance, or even if in good faith, the dispensation is invalid: this Reiffenstuel asserts to be the unanimous and certain doctrine.[46]

tamen si prudenter ac bona fide judicaverit Praelatus causam esse justam, quae alias talis non erat. Immo licite dispensabit quamvis dubitet utrum causa dispensationis sit justa."

[44] *Tractatus de Sacramento Matrimonii* (Venetiis, 1756), Lib. VIII, c. 14, n. 7: "Quod adeo verum est ut, quamvis praelatus inferior bona fide procedat existimans esse justam causam, dispensatio sit nulla."

[45] Cf. Reiffenstuel, *Jus Canonicum Universum, Appendix ad Quartum Librum,* § V, n. 204.

[46] *Jus Canonicum Universum, Appendix ad Quartum Librum,* § V, n. 206: "Falsitas circa causam motivam seu finalem etiam ex simplicitate vel ignorantia commissa vitiat et nullam reddit dispensationem. Unanimis et certa"; also, *Theologia Moralis,* Tract. II, dist. 4, n. 22, additio: "Ex quo colliges, quod dispensatio sit invalida si dispensandus in sua supplicia allegat causam motivam seu finalem a parte rei falsam, quamvis id etiam bona fide et ex inculpabili ignorantia faceret, putans illam causam allegatem esse a parte rei veram." — Cf. also Schmalzgrueber, *Jus Ecclesiasticum Universum,* 5 vols. in 12 (Romae, 1843-1845) Lib. IV, Pars 3, tit. 16, § 5, n. 150.

# PART II

# CANONICAL COMMENTARY

# CHAPTER VI

# CAUSES FOR DISPENSATIONS

## Article 1. Kinds of Causes

Whenever the cause for a dispensation is considered, the question of the quality of the cause is of utmost importance since not all causes exert equal influence upon the dispensing authority, nor do they all possess the import necessary to gain a dispensation. The causes may be viewed from different aspects and the species will vary according to the point of view from which they are considered.

When dispensations in general are considered, the alleged cause as viewed from the aspect of its influence upon the dispensing authority can be either motivating (final) or impulsive (accessory). The motivating or final cause[1] is one which of itself induces the dispensing authority to grant the dispensation which is being sought, since it sufficiently moves the reasoning of the dispensing authority to conclude that it is justifiable to dispense in this particular case. It is actually the reason why the dispensing authority acts and should it not have been presented to his consideration, the dispensation most likely would not have been granted or it would have been granted conditionally.[2] An impulsive or accessory cause, on the other hand, is a secondary cause which of itself does not suffice to influence the dispensing authority to grant the dispensation but it helps to convince the one in authority that a dispensation is justifiable. It adds weight to the alleged final cause so that the one in authority finds it easier to grant the dispensation, but even if it had not been submitted for consideration, the dispensing agent would nonetheless have granted the favor. It adds only to the facility with which the dispensing authority grants the relaxation from the law.[3]

1 Canons 42, § 2, 45, 86.

2 Cf. Reiffenstuel, *Jus Canonicum Universum,* Lib. I, tit. 3, n. 183; De Justis, *De Dispensationibus Matrimonialibus,* Lib. III, c. I, n. 46; Cicognani-Staffa, II, 345.

3 Cf. Reiffenstuel, *loc. cit.;* Sanchez, *De Sancto Matrimonii Sacramento,* Lib. III, c. I, n. 53; Cicognani-Staffa, *loc. cit.*

The motivating or final causes are determined either by law or by the practice of the Roman Curia, and these are called canonical causes. The canonical causes for matrimonial dispensations were listed by the Sacred Congregation for the Propagation of the Faith[4] and later were amplified by the Apostolic Datary,[5] but these lists are not all inclusive nor do they refer to other than matrimonial dispensations. To grant dispensations from the ecclesiastical laws, where no norm nor list is given to determine whether the alleged cause is a motivating one or not, and it cannot be determined from the practice of the Roman Curia, then it remains for the prudent judgment of the dispensing authority to decide. He can arrive at his conclusion only after taking into consideration the common law, and the practice and custom invoked under similar circumstances.[6]

A motivating or an impulsive cause may be said to be intrinsic or extrinsic in relation to the law from which a dispensation is sought. An intrinsic cause is one which is directly opposed to the observation of the law, since it renders the obligation to the law very burdensome, or a greater good evolves when the observance of the law is not imposed in a particular case. Thus a long bumpy journey to Church for an elderly person to fulfill the precept of assisting at Sunday Mass is burdensome; so also is the observance of fast for a person who is weakened by illness. An extrinsic cause is one which arises from some more general advantage derived from the relaxation of the law. It does not emanate directly from the opposition to the observance of the law but rather stems from some external circumstances, as for example, the rank of nobility of the petitioner; or the authority desires to reward the special merits of an individual or of a specific community; or to avoid the occasion of numerous transgressions of the law, as when a legal holiday falls on a Friday and the

[4] Cf. Instructio, 9 maii 1877—*Collectanea S.C. de Prop. Fide,* n. 1470; *Fontes,* n. 4890.

[5] Cf. *ASS,* XXXIV (1901-1902), 34-35.

[6] Cf. Reiffenstuel, *Jus Canonicum Universum,* Lib. I, tit. 3, n. 195; Sanchez, *De Sancto Matrimonii Sacramento,* Lib. VIII, disp. 21, n. 19.

bishop dispenses from the obligation of the law of fast and abstinence.[7]

The cause may also be considered in relation to whose good is intended by the dispensation. Such a cause is public when the entire community reaps the benefit which results from the dispensation of the law, whereas a private cause benefits only the individual or individuals for whom the relaxation of the law was granted. Although a public cause is not demanded in the present discipline, nevertheless the private cause should be such that a dispensation granted under its influence, will at least indirectly be beneficial to the common good.

### Article 2. Causes for Dispensations in Proportion to the Gravity of the Law

Canon 84, § 1, stipulates that a just and reasonable cause must be present before a lawful and valid dispensation can be granted by a subordinate dispensing agent, adding that this cause must be in due proportion to the gravity of the law which has been relaxed in a particular case. In this wise, the Code of Canon Law imposes the obligation upon the dispensing authority to counterbalance the alleged causes with the gravity of the obligation of the law: the greater the obligation, the greater the cause required.[8] Naturally this cannot be accomplished in a material and physical manner, but only by the prudent judgment of the dispensing authority.

Wherever the Code of Canon Law concedes the faculty to dispense, the different qualities of the necessary causes are usually listed. The legislator, designating the various degrees in the causes necessary for a dispensation, underscores the fact that there is a gradation in the obligation imposed by the law from which a dispensation is sought. This is clearly shown

[7] Cf. Suarez, *De Legibus,* Lib. VI, c. 18, n. 24; — Opera Omnia, Vol. VI, p. 89; Michiels, *Normae Generales,* II, 742; Van Hove, *De Privilegiis; De Dispensationibus,* n. 452.

[8] Suarez, *De Legibus,* Lib. VI, c. 18, n. 16: "Ubi fuerit major obligatio, ibi major causa postulatur."—Opera Omnia, vol. VI, p. 87.

in the canons stipulating that either a legitimate (canon 1028, § 1), a just (v.g. canons 1245, § 1, 291, § 1 etc.) a grave (canons 465, § 2, 972, § 1), a just and grave (canon 1061, § 1, n. 1), a grave and reasonable (canon 755, § 2), a grave and urgent (canon 735, § 2), a special (canon 564, § 1), or a most grave and most urgent (canon 1104) cause be present before a relaxation from that particular law could possibly be granted. This does not connote, however, that a just cause need not be a legitimate cause, or that a grave cause need not be a just one, since every alleged cause for a dispensation must be just and reasonable. The degree of the gravity of the cause must always be judged in proportion to the gravity of the law. This is made quite apparent by canon 84, § 1, and it applies to all causes which are brought forth in quest of a dispensation, and the grantor of a dispensation must abide by this norm. Consequently the causes cannot be examined as something apart from the law, in an absolute or abstract manner, but the ratio between the gravity of the law and the gravity of the cause must be determined as the norm which will guide the dispensing agent either to grant or refuse the requested favor.

If the alleged cause, then, is to be considered in proportion to the gravity of the law, it stands to reason that the cause must exist objectively. The dispensing agent, to act reasonably, weighs the objective facts which confront him in order that he may render a prudent decision. That the law exists, is taken for granted here as it must be taken for granted by the one who is requested to grant a dispensation from the obligation of that law. The question to be decided by the dispensing authority is whether or not the ratio between the obligation and the cause exists. His common denominator, as it were, is *gravitas*. If the cause does not exist objectively or if it is erroneously believed to exist, then the objective proportion cannot be ascertained nor determined. In order to determine the proportion between two entities, as specified by the legislator, they must both exist objectively, otherwise the equilibrium of the balance cannot be viewed objectively. The judgment of the dispensing agent is moved by the alleged cause which must be based on realities otherwise the judgment will not be based on things as they really exist. The judgment of the dispensing agent is not merely speculative but must be a practical and prudent judgment based on realities. This could not result from an erroneous judgment that a cause exists where it really and objectively does not, because a non-existent being could not be placed in juxta-position with an existing entity. In other words, a non-existent cause cannot be compared to a positively existent law in order to determine whether or not a due proportion between the two exists. Consequently, if the alleged cause does not exist in fact, that is, objectively, but is either proferred with false allegations, even if in good faith, or is believed erroneously to exist, the conditions set down by canon 84, § 1 are not fulfilled. The actual juridic effect upon a dispensation granted under such circumstances will be discussed in the next article.

The good faith of the petitioners as well as the good faith of the grantor will have no juridic effects upon the dispensations; good faith concerns the morality of an action. Should a dispensation be granted in a case where it ought not to have been, the good faith of all concerned will absolve each of any moral blame in accordance to each one's good faith. The good faith, however, does not bring into being that which actually does not exist juridically; and if a just cause does not exist, all the good faith in the world will not give it birth. Good faith does not produce causes where there are none.

### *Section A. Legitimate cause* (legitima causa)

The alleged cause for any dispensation must be a legitimate one even though the wording *legitima causa* is rarely found in the Code of Canon Law. To be legitimate the cause must necessarily be a truthful and real cause, not one which emanated from someone's imagination. A legitimate cause is one which conforms to the accepted standard norms which regulate the granting of dispensations. Pope Benedict XIV commenting upon the faculties of the bishops to dispense from banns before a marriage reminds the bishops that it behooves them to keep in mind the restraints of prudence and the norms of good judgment; which is the same as to require a legitimate cause.[9]

This regulation requiring a legitimate cause for the dispensation from the publication of the banns prior to the celebration of a marriage has been incorporated into the Code of Canon Law in canon 1028, § 1, which affords a good example for the purpose of examining a *causa legitima*. The reason why the law requires the publication of the banns is obviously to determine the freedom of the parties concerned from any impediment to their proposed marriage. This law is a general one and it imposes a grave obligation.[10]

In order to determine whether the alleged cause in a petition for a dispensation from the banns is a legitimate one, various circumstances must be considered before the dispensing agent can arrive at a decision whether the cause is proportionate to the gravity of the law demanding the publication of the banns. Should the spouses-to-be come from the same parish and be known personally to the pastor, the cause need not be as grave as for a couple, one of whom comes from another parish and is unknown to the priest who is to assist at the marriage. This cause in turn need not be as grave as in a case wherein one of the parties comes from a distant city or State, or even from another country. If both of the future spouses are known personally by the pastor and he is absolutely certain there is no impediment to their marriage, the cause for a dispensation need not be a serious one, since the purpose of the law is fulfilled without the actual and absolute need for the publication of the banns.[11]

[9] Ep. encycl. *Satis Vobis,* 17 nov. 1741, § 5: ". . . haec tamen facilitas [dispensandi] non a sola dispensantis voluntate pendet, sed a Tridentino coercetur arctis prudentiae, discretisque arbitrii legibus; quod idem est, ac legitimam causam dispensationis requirere."—*Fontes,* n. 319.

[10] Cf. Sanchez, *De Sancto Matrimonii Sacramento,* Lib. III, disp. 5, n. 6; St. Alphonsus, *Theologia Moralis,* Lib. VI, n. 990; Gasparri, *De Matrimonio,* I, n. 150; Cappello, *De Sacramentis,* V, n. 161.

[11] Cf. Sanchez, *De Sancto Matrimonii Sacramento,* Lib. III, disp. 9, n. 3; St. Alphonsus, *Theologia Moralis,* Lib. VI, n. 1006; Cappello, *De Sacramentis,*

Such would not be the case should one of the parties be unknown to the pastor or the priest who is to assist at the marriage. A grave cause would be demanded before a dispensation could be lawfully and validly granted. Naturally a more serious cause would be needed for a dispensation from three banns than from two or just one publication of the banns. When there is no previous certitude as to the freedom of the parties from any impediments, some serious cause must be present. Amongst those causes which would be considered as legitimate, would be the fact that the groom is forced to undertake a long journey or is being sent on military tour of duty and the couple desires to be married before his departure, there being no time to make even one proclamation of the banns. Similarly, the cause would be legitimate if there is a question of revalidating a marriage which has been contracted before a civil magistrate, especially if the parties have lived together for many years in this manner while the rest of the community believed them to be validly married; or if the contracting parties are of the nobility or of high rank in government circles, because then such persons would be well known and should there be any impediments it would have been public knowledge; or if the difference in the ages would leave the couple subject to derision.[12] If both contractants are unknown to the priest and a serious reason does not exist for a dispensation from three banns, it could not be granted unless a supplementary oath as to their *status liber* was made by them.

For a dispensation from two or one publications of banns, any good reason why the marriage date must be hastened would be a legitimate cause; such as, if after the publication of one bann, there is danger that the parents would unreason-

V, n. 168; *contra* De Smet, who contends: "Etiam ad dispensandum super una vel duplici proclamatione, non est nimia facilitate utendum, ita ut solus nuptrientium lubitus pro causa, quantumvis aliunde moraliter constat de impedimenti absentia: est enim lex, eaque fundata in praesumptione periculi universalis." — *De Sponsalibus et Matrimonio,* n. 64.

12 Cf. Sanchez, *De Sancto Matrimonii Sacramento,* Lib. III, disp. 9; Cappello, *De Sacramentis,* V, n. 168.

ably withdraw their previously granted consent, or if there is any danger of scandal, or danger that the marriage may be unjustly impeded or delayed.

The legitimacy of the cause must be decided by the dispensing authority after taking into consideration the law itself and the circumstances and reasons why the dispensation is desired. After due, but not judicial, investigation, he must decide with prudence and in accordance to the law whether the proposed cause is in proportion to the law from which the dispensation is sought. If in his prudent estimation the proportion is present, he then concedes the dispensation; otherwise he must refuse to grant the favor and insist upon the fulfillment of the law lest its purpose be frustrated.

### *Section B. Just cause* (iusta causa)

The question as to what constitutes a just cause is not an easy one to answer. It is not a concept which can be considered absolutely, and a definite measure cannot be supplied or established to determine that one or the other cause is a just one for all dispensations. Just cause is a relative concept: the relation between the alleged cause and the law from which the dispensation is sought. A just cause must be in conformity to the law, according to the rules of equity. A prudent examination of circumstances as well as the causes must be made by the dispensing authority before he can rightfully judge the justice of a given cause.[13]

In order to aid the dispensing agent to arrive at a prudent decision in accordance to his conscience as to the justice of the alleged cause which has been presented to be scrutinized by him, there are certain norms which he must keep in mind. A just cause will also be a sufficient cause for a dispensation. Now to determine the sufficiency of a cause, and *a fortiori* the justice of a cause, the dispensing authority takes into consideration: 1. the necessity of the dispensation, whether the necessity be public or private, in other words, will this dispensation enhance the common good or at least the individu-

[13] Cf. Cicognani-Staffa, II, 617; Michiels, *Normae Generales*, II, 472-473.

al's welfare;[14] 2. charity, whether the dispensation will be of value to the spiritual well-being of the individual or individuals in whose benefit the dispensation is granted, and the benefit which will accrue to the community as a whole, as for example, peace between States or nations.[15] To be a just cause it need not possess the proportions of cause which would excuse from the observance of the law, because then no dispensation need be sought. A just cause need be only a *causa media,* which would be sufficient to subtract an individual from the obligation of the law without, however, showing any favoritism for any particular person.[16]

Since a just cause must be considered in relation to the law from which a dispensation is to be granted, other elements must enter into the deliberation. The first and most important is the gravity of the law itself, then the importance of the people concerned, and the present practice of the Roman Curia.[17] The gravity of the law, however, is judged not merely from the fact that the law which is to suffer a relaxation imposed a grave obligation, but also from the gravity of the harm that the common good must suffer by the relaxation of the obligation.[18] Consequently both of these elements must be taken into consideration by the dispensing agent while he debates whether the gravity of the cause is in proportion to the gravity of the law. Furthermore, he must also consider the possibility of scandal which may arise from the concession of the dispensation, and on the other hand, the possibility of serious scandal which may result should the dispensation be refused.

[14] Cf. Suarez, *De Legibus,* Lib. VI, c. 18, n. 18 — *Opera Omnia,* VI, p. 87.

[15] Cf. Cicognani-Staffa, II, 618; Bouquillon, *Theologia Moralis Fundamentalis* (2 ed., Ratisbonae, Cinn., Neo Eboraci: Pustet, 1890), n. 174, p. 376; Michiels, *Normae Generales,* II, 744-745; Brys, *De Dispensationibus in Iure Canonico,* p. 188.

[16] Cf. Suarez, *De Legibus,* Lib. VI, c. 18, n. 14 — *Opera Omnia,* VI, p. 86.

[17] Cf. Payen, *De Matrimonio in Missionibus ac Potissimum in Sinis* (Zi-ka-wek: Typographia T'OU-SE-WE, 1935-1936), I, n. 730 (hereafter cited *De Matrimonio*).

[18] Cf. Bouquillon, *Theologia Moralis Fundamentalis,* n. 174, p. 374.

There is no doubt that some laws impose a graver obligation than others. This is true not only for marriage legislation, but for other fields included in the Code of Canon Law. Thus to dispense from the impediment of consanguinity in the second degree of the collateral line, a much graver cause is demanded than for a dispensation from the impediment in the third degree of the collateral line; a graver cause is needed for a dispensation from a diriment impediment than from impeding impediments, otherwise it could not be said to be just and in accordance to the ratio demanded by the legislator.

Digressing from legislation pertaining to marriage impediments to other laws which demand a just cause for a dispensation, one can discover that the pastor is obliged to preach a homily to his parishioners every Sunday and Holy Day of Obligation.[19] He cannot habitually satisfy this obligation by a substitute unless a just reason is present and is approved by the bishop.[20] This approbation by the bishop is in effect a dispensation from the general law which forbids pastors habitually to shirk their duty of preaching. The obligation of the law is a grave one, since it is the grave duty of the pastor having the care of souls as his responsibility, to keep them instructed in spiritual matters and to do so personally.[21] Just and proportionate reasons which would be in proportion to the gravity of the obligation imposed by canon 1344, would be, for example, the failing memory of the pastor, or some chronic throat ailment which would make it difficult for him to preach regularly.

Another example: the local Ordinary and the pastor have the faculty to dispense in a particular case and for a just reason from the general law of observance of the precept to

19 Canon 1344, § 1.

20 Canon 1344, § 2.

21 Cf. Coronata, *Institutiones Iuris Canonici,* II, 928; Koudelka, *Pastors, Their Rights and Obligations,* The Catholic University of America Canon Law Studies, n. 11 (Washington, D. C.: The Catholic University of America, 1921), p. 61.

hear Mass on Sundays and Holy Days of Obligation.[22] No one denies the gravity of the obligation imposed by the law demanding the observance of this precept. It is difficult to determine exactly just how grave the just cause must be to justify a dispensation from this law. One thing is certain: the cause for the dispensation will be less grave than one which will excuse from the law. One may be excused from the precept of hearing Mass on the days prescribed for a moderately grave reason, such as notable inconvenience or notable harm, charity shown by taking care of the sick, etc., so a less grave cause may suffice for a dispensation. This cause, however, must not be so light as to lose sight of the gravity of the precept.[23] It certainly would not be a just cause for a pastor to dispense someone from the precept to hear Mass on Sunday so that this person could apply himself to the preparation of a parish picnic. The proportion between the cause and the gravity of the law would not be a just one, and furthermore, the parishioners would be justifiably scandalized by such procedure.

The second element to be taken into consideration when judging the justice of the cause, is the importance of the parties concerned. A dispensation granted to members of the royalty need not have as grave a cause because of the apparent good which may ensue for the entire nation: peace may be enhanced or peaceful relations between countries may be re-established.

Thirdly, the practice of the Roman Curia plays a prominent role in discerning which cause can be accepted as a just one for a particular dispensation. Demonstrative lists have been drawn up by the Sacred Congregation for the Propagation of the Faith[24] and the Apostolic Datary,[25] for matrimonial

22 Canon 1245, § 1.

23 Cf. Guiniven, *The Precept of Hearing Mass,* The Catholic University of America Canon Law Studies, n. 158 (Washington, D. C.: The Catholic University of America Press, 1942), p. 161.

24 Cf. Instr., 9 maii 1877 — *Collectanea, S. C. de Prop. Fide,* n. 1470; *Fontes,* n. 4890; and also the excellent examination of these causes by O'Mara, *Canonical Causes for Matrimonial Dispensations,* The Catholic University of

dispensations. These causes are considered as just and sufficient for the majority of the dispensations from matrimonial impediments. They are not, however, to be considered as just and sufficient for all the impediments. The Sacred Congregation of the Sacraments, for example, gave notice that the causes which normally would suffice for a matrimonial dispensation would hardly suffice for a dispensation from the impediment of consanguinity in the second degree in the collateral line mixed with the first. A much graver cause must be submitted before it can be considered as just and sufficient, such as: the removal of notable scandal, the settlement of serious differences arising from testate succession of goods in the family, or to alleviate the very wretched conditions of the families.[26]

### *Section C. Reasonable cause* (rationabilis causa)

Every positive law is an ordinance or regulation of reason promulgated by the head of the community for the sake of the common welfare of that community. As such it must be observed by every member of the community. A dispensation on the other hand, is a relaxation from the ordinance of reason in favor of one or more individuals.[27] Since the relaxation tends to show a special favor for some while seemingly ignor-

America Canon Law Studies, n. 96 (Washington, D. C.: The Catholic University of America, 1935), pp. 69-130.

[25] Cf. *ASS,* XXXIV (1901-1902), 34-35.

[26] S. C. de Sacramentis, instr., 1 aug. 1931: "Eas proinde solummodo iustas et congruenter graves habeant causas Exmi Praesules in memoratis dispensationibus efflagitandas, quae ob canonicas praescriptiones, aut ob diuturnum usum iugiter a S. Sede servatum, uti legitimae aestimantur, prout sunt v. g. remotio scandali, compositio gravium quaestionum in successione bonorum, aut resolutio implexarum vel valde miserarum conditionum familiarum. Ideoque ad rem haud sufficere censeant suetas, quae pro ceteris impedimentis etiam maioris gradus adducuntur, causas: nempe angustiam loci, aetatem mulieris superadultam, carentiam dotis et similia, excepto casu quo eadem, non singillatim sed cumulativae sumptae, tam grave pondus efforment, ut dispensationem suadent, iuxta regulam iuris 'singula quae non prosunt, simul collecta iuvant'."—*AAS,* XXIII (1931), 414-415.

[27] Canon 80.

ing the other members of the community, an inequality of treatment of the members by the one in authority results. This inequality must be explained, otherwise the complaints of those not affected by the relaxation would be entirely justified and the grantor could be accused of undue partiality in his dealings with his subjects. Consequently to exonerate the governing authority for the apparent partiality, the motives for his action must be examined. If it is discovered that his actions were in accordance with reason, in other words, if it is found, after examining the motives and the law which was relaxed, that any prudent man would have acted in the same manner, the dispensing authority would be said to have acted reasonably.[28] The examination would prove that there was just as much reason why some were dispensed from the law in a particular case as there was for all the other members to abide by that law.

A reasonable cause at first sight may appear to be one which is a minor and not a very serious cause. It is true that in some instances the reasonable cause demanded by some canons will not be a serious or grave one. This is so only because the law from which a reasonable cause would excuse does not impose a grave obligation or because the common good would not suffer any serious harm by the relaxation of that law in a particular instance. Canon 1030, § 1, requires a reasonable cause to permit a marriage to take place within less than three days after the last of the banns have been published. Once the grave obligation of publishing the banns is fulfilled, the free status of the parties is established and all the other pertinent documents are on hand, the obligation of the three day delay does not seem to be a serious one. Even a slight cause, though a reasonable one, will be sufficient to permit the marriage a day or two after the last bann is published.[29]

This however cannot be taken as a general rule that a reasonable cause is always a slight cause or any cause at all.

[28] Cf. Suarez, *De Legibus,* Lib. VI, c. 18, n. 26—*Opera Omnia,* VI, p. 90.
[29] Cf. Cappello, *De Sacramentis,* V, n. 181.

If the obligation of the law is not a grave one, then neither will the reasonable cause be a grave one; but if the obligation of the law is a grave one, then the reasonable cause will also be a grave one. This is illustrated by canon 859, § 1: every Catholic who has reached the age of reason is under the grave obligation to receive the Holy Eucharist at least once a year, unless for some reasonable cause upon the advice of the pastor this obligation is deferred temporarily. A child, then, who reaches the age of reason is bound by this law and only a proportionately grave cause will suffice to postpone for a short time his first reception of Holy Communion. The desire of the parents to have their child receive the First Holy Communion only with other children of the class, which would entail a delay of a year, cannot be considered a reasonable cause; nor could a local custom of permitting children to receive only after they attained the age of nine, be a reasonable cause. A few months delay, in order that the recipient may be better prepared for the first Holy Communion by imparting greater knowledge and arousing greater devotion for its reception, would be a grave enough cause: it is a grave obligation to be properly prepared and disposed for the reception of the Holy Communion.[30]

### *Section D. Just and reasonable cause* (iusta et rationabilis causa)

After the concept of a just cause and the concept of a reasonable cause have been examined separately, the concept of a just and reasonable cause deserves some consideration because canon 84, § 1 imposed the precept that no dispensation may be granted unless a *just and reasonable* cause is present and is in proportion to the gravity of the law which is relaxed. The reasonableness of a cause adds little to the concept of a just cause: to be a just cause it also must be a reasonable one. It affords added emphasis to the fact that a proportion between the alleged cause and the gravity of the

[30] Cf. Cappello, *De Sacramentis,* I (ed. 5, Taurini - Romae: Marietti, 1947), n. 425.

law must be considered and examined prudently and with equity. The concept of reasonableness in conjunction with the justice of the cause rather gives the norm by which the justice of the cause is determined. Is this just and reasonable cause a grave one, or is it a minor and slight cause? That will depend upon the gravity of the law to be dispensed. One thing is certain, every cause which is advanced in a petition for a dispensation for any and every law from which a dispensation may be granted either by the legislator or some other dispensing agent receiving this faculty from the legislator, must be a just and reasonable one.[31]

Even though a permission is not a dispensation, the causes for a permission must have the same proportion to the law as the causes for a dispensation, and the same rule of proportion obtains, analogically, for each.[32] To better illustrate that a just and reasonable cause is not merely a slight or minor cause but can be a grave one, canon 1402, § 2 offers a good example. If the Ordinary has been granted a general faculty by the Holy See to permit his subjects to retain and read forbidden books, he shall grant this permission with discretion and for just and reasonable causes. The law forbidding the reading of prohibited books imposes a grave obligation because the pernicious books present a grave danger to faith and morals. The just and reasonable cause, then, must be proportionately grave before permission can be given to retain and read such books. Among such serious causes are included: scientific research for the purpose of furthering the cause of the Church by exposing and refuting contradicting teachings and errors; the study of schismatic or heretical errors by seminary or university professors in order to give the necessary criticism in their explanations; students who may be

31 Canon 84, § 1.

32 Although the Code of Canon Law gives no specific norm to govern the granting of permissions as it does for the granting of dispensations, the norm of canon 84, § 1, can be applied to the causes required for permissions, in view of the prescription of canon 20: "Si certa de re desit expressum praescriptum legis sive generalis sive particularis, norma sumenda est, nisi agatur de poenis applicandis, a legibus latis in similibus."

engaged in a specialized study which will entail the consultation of books otherwise prohibited.

Another example wherein the law requires a just and reasonable cause before a permission may be granted is the extraordinary case in which a bishop may permit a marriage between two Catholics to take place in a private home.[33] Two conditions, however, must be verified. The case must not be one which occurs frequently, consequently, the bishop could not grant a general permission to a certain group or even to a certain family. The second condition is that a proportionate cause must be present. A very urgent or grave cause does not seem to be required: such as a serious illness which would prevent one of the parties to be transported to a church. A sufficient cause which would be just and reasonable is the necessity to convalidate secretly a marriage which is invalid because of some impediment unknown to the general public, or if there is some difficulty in getting to a church because of the inconvenience of distance.[34] The nature of this law is such that it does not seem to impose a grave obligation nor does the common good suffer any great harm by its relaxation. Consequently, although the cause for the permission must be a proportionate one it need not be a grave one.

### *Section E. Grave cause* (gravis causa)

The legislator has explicitly indicated that certain laws can be relaxed only for grave reasons. In this way, the specified law is designated by the legislator as a serious one, imposing a serious obligation, the disobedience to which would constitute grave harm to the common welfare. Even though a variance of terminology is encountered in the Code of Canon Law, as for example: grave cause (e.g. canons 465 § 2, 1269 § 3 amongst others), a just and grave cause (e.g. canon 464 § 2, 1061 § 1 n. 1) and grave and reasonable cause (canon 755 § 2), there will be no difference in the quality of the cause. Even though not every just and reasonable cause is a

33 Canon 1109, § 2.

34 Cf. Payen, *De Matrimonio,* II, n. 1959-bis.

grave one, every grave cause must be both just and reasonable, otherwise it would not fulfill the demands of canon 84, § 1. The gravity of the law, then, determines the gravity of the required cause; circumstances of time, place and persons, as well as the scandal which may result should the dispensation be granted or if it should not be granted also enter into the consideration when determining the gravity of the cause in relation to the grave obligation imposed by the law from which a dispensation is sought.

For the sake of clarity, a few of the laws requiring a grave cause for a relaxation or for a permission will be analyzed to show how the ratio between the cause and the law must be observed. The general law prescribes that the Holy Eucharist must be preserved in a permanently fixed tabernacle located in the center of the altar.[35] This is a grave precept, since it is a grave duty to care for the Most Blessed Eucharist, guarding it most carefully and preserving it from all profanation.[36] Before the Blessed Sacrament could be perserved outside the tabernacle as prescribed by law, certain definite conditions must be verified. A grave cause must be present, and it must be approved by the bishop. Only then is it allowed to remove the Holy Eucharist from the tabernacle during the night, provided that it is decently placed on a corporal and kept in a proper and safer place than is afforded by the tabernacle,[37] and there must be at least one vigil light burning before the Blessed Sacrament thus preserved.[38] The grave causes which suffice for the bishop to permit and at times to demand that the Blessed Sacrament be safely preserved outside the tabernacle are: to avoid the grave danger of theft which would expose the Sacred Species to sacrilegious profanation; and, to afford greater safety during times of war especially during the night air attacks.[39] The danger of theft must be a grave danger, not merely the ordinary danger which may be said to

[35] Canon 1269, § 1.

[36] S. C. de Sacramentis, instr., 26 maii 1938—*AAS*, XXX (1938), 198.

[37] Canon 1269, § 3.

[38] Canon 1271.

[39] Cf. S. C. de Sacramentis, ep., 15 sept. 1943—*AAS* XXXV (1943), 284.

exist at all times. If after all the ordinary precautions indicated by the Sacred Congregation of the Sacraments[40] are taken, and the danger is still prudently considered to exist, then the Holy Eucharist can be preserved for the night in a safer place. All the other regulations for such safe-keeping outside the tabernacle, however, must be carefully fulfilled.

Another law which stipulates that a grave cause is needed for its relaxation is the one which obliges a pastor to personal residence within his parish.[41] This obligation arises from the very nature of his office which entails the care of the souls of all his parishioners.[42] The reason for this obligation is obviously to insure that the necessary vigilance and direction of the spiritual welfare of the faithful is properly effected. The gravity of this obligation of residence in accordance with the law, is clearly indicated in the Council of Trent. After indicating that the bishops are bound to residence under the pain of mortal sin, "absolutely the same as regards the guilt . . . does the holy council declare and decree with reference to those of lower rank and to all others who hold any ecclesiastical benefice to whom is entrusted the care of the souls."[43] Only one of the ways by which the pastor can violate this law need be considered here for our purposes, namely, a prolonged absence from the parish over and above the two months which is permitted by law. The bishop may permit a longer absence or shorten the time of absence for a grave reason.[44]

The Council of Trent lists four basic reasons why one having the care of souls as his trust, could absent himself with due permission for a longer period of time than that permitted by law. These are: Christian charity, urgent necessity, due

[40] Instr., 26 maii 1938 — *AAS,* XXX (1938), 201-202.

[41] Canon 465, § 1.

[42] Canon 464, § 1.

[43] "Eadem omnino, etiam quoad culpam . de curatis inferioribus et aliis quibuscumque, qui beneficium aliquod ecclesiasticum curam animarum habens obtinet sacrosancta synodus declarat et decernit." — Sess. XXIII, *de ref.*, c. 1.

[44] Canon 465, § 2.

obedience and manifest advantage to the Church or State.[45] All of these causes, however, must be judged in proportion to the harm which the faithful in his care may possibly suffer by his absence. If the absence of the pastor is effectively supplanted by a substitute while the pastor leads a pilgrimage to some distant shrine causing him to be away from his own parishioners for more than two months: this would be a cause grave enough to permit the absence by the bishop. However, this could not be an annual occurrence, for although it may be Christian charity to lead pilgrimages to religious shrines, it would cease to be in proportion to the pastor's primary obligation to his own flock. His annual absence of four to five months would be a neglect of the welfare of those entrusted to his care. Other causes which are considered grave enough would be the ill-health of the pastor requiring medical treatment for a longer time; the absence due to obedience to the pope or one's proper bishop while performing a special mission which requires a lengthy absence; or when a pastor acts as a delegate to a Plenary Council or a Synod; or when he strives to obtain relief for his locality during an emergency.[46] It is presumed that in each instance, besides the presence of a grave cause, the permission of the bishop as well as his approval of the substitute is obtained. If the presence of the pastor is essential to settle some problem the bishop may even foreshorten the two months absence that is permitted the pastor by law.

In the legislation concerning matrimonial impediments, the Code of Canon Law indicates the necessity of a just and grave cause for a dispensation from the impediments of mixed religion and disparity of cult.[47] The gravity of the law prohibiting such marriages stems not only from the nature of the causes required for the dispensation but also from the fact that the Church saw fit to enact a special norm indicating the

[45] Sess. XXIII, *de ref.*, c. 1.

[46] Cf. Reilly, *Residence of Pastors*, The Catholic University of America Canon Law Studies, n. 97 (Washington, D. C.: The Catholic University of America, 1935), pp. 40-42.

[47] Canons 1061, § 1, n. 1, and 1071.

gravity of this law: the Church most severely prohibits marriages between a Catholic and a non-Catholic. But even before the dispensation can be granted there must be moral certitude that the danger of perversion of the Catholic party and the children who may be born of that wedlock, is removed; otherwise the marriage would be forbidden by divine law.[48] The dangers, then, of a mixed marriage are such that the Church is reluctant to permit the Catholic to undertake the risks unless there are just and grave reasons for doing so. The grave causes are required over and above the usual *cautiones* given by both the Catholic and the non-Catholic promising that all the children will be baptized and reared in the Catholic faith, that the non-Catholic will respect the freedom of action of the Catholic in fulfilling religious duties, and that all danger of perversion of the faith is absent.

The Code of Canon Law does not specify which causes are to be considered as just and grave, for that reason recourse must be had to the causes proposed as canonical by the Sacred Congregation for the Propagation of the Faith and the Roman Datary. The gravity of these causes, however, is not to be judged absolutely, but rather relatively, bearing in mind the circumstances of time and place.[49] Even these causes, though indicated as canonical, will not readily suffice when taken singly unless there are other circumstances which provide added weight and gravity to the alleged cause, or when two of the causes are present simultaneously.[50] Although the Church no longer demands public causes, but is more lenient and accepts private causes, the public good must still be taken into consideration. The private causes, such as, the smallness of the place, the lack of a dowry, the superadult age of the Catholic woman etc., are not of themselves generally in proportion to the grave danger to which the Catholic party

[48] Canon 1060.

[49] Cf. Cappello, *De Sacramentis,* V, n. 314.

[50] Cf. Cappello, *loc. cit.;* De Smet, *De Sponsalibus et Matrimonio,* n. 506; Wernz-Vidal, *Ius Canonicum,* V (ed. 3, a P. Aguirre recognita, Romae: Apud Aedes Universitatis Gregorianae, 1946), n. 178, nota 30, p. 207.

and the children are exposed, except in cases wherein the danger can be prudently said to be non-existent.[51]

Which causes, then, can be looked upon as sufficiently grave to gain a dispensation from the impediment of mixed religion or disparity of cult? A slight or minor cause will hardly suffice: the fact that the engaged couple are "madly in love" is not a cause for the dispensation. Such a cause has never received the approval of the Holy See nor is it listed amongst the generally accepted causes; it has rather been explicitly rejected.[52] Some of the causes which are regarded as sufficiently grave by the more recent authors are: the predominance of non-Catholics in a particular region wherein there is no hindrance or hostility toward the religious freedom for Catholics; if the marriage is the only solution by which children born of a previous mixed marriage can be reared in the Catholic faith; if otherwise a grave public scandal would result from the pregnancy, or defamation, and this cannot be avoided except by permitting a mixed marriage; if there is danger of apostasy; the convalidation of a civil ceremony with a non-Catholic if the Catholic party is sincerely penitent and seeks reconciliation with the Church, especially with the desire of Catholic Baptism for any children born of such wedlock; if there is probable hope that a non-Catholic family will enter the Church through the mixed marriage; if there is hope of conversion of the non-Catholic party, and even more so if there is a written promise of the non-Catholic to become a convert after the marriage; and the danger of marriage before a civil magistrate or a non-Catholic minister.[53]

[51] Cf. Ter Haar, *De Matrimoniis Mixtis Eorumque Remediis* (Taurini-Romae: Marietti, 1931), n. 62.

[52] Cf. Benedictus XIV, Declaratio *Matrimonia,* 4 nov. 1741, § 3 — *Fontes,* n. 3527.

[53] Cf. Ter Haar, *op. cit.,* n. 64; Cappello, *De Sacramentis,* V, n. 314; De Smet, *De Sponsalibus et Matrimonio,* n. 506; Bangen, *Instructio Practica de Sponsalibus et Matrimonio* (4 vols. in 1, Monasterii, 1858-1860), Tit. IV, pp. 20-21; Schenk, *Matrimonial Impediments of Mixed Religion and Disparity of Cult,* The Catholic University of America Canon Law Studies, n. 51 (Washington, D. C.: The Catholic University of America, 1929), pp. 197-198.

In all of these cases, a public cause will quite naturally have greater import than a private cause, but this does not permit one to conclude that only public causes are grave causes. Whether one cause is considered to be graver than the next matters little. The main requirement for a lawful and valid dispensation by a subordinate dispensing agent is that the alleged cause be sufficiently grave to be in proportion to the gravity of the law from which a dispensation is sought. The prudent judgment concerning the gravity and the proportion is the responsibility of the dispensing agent, the practice of the Roman Curia and the circumstances existing in each particular locality having been taken duly into consideration.

*Section F. Most grave cause* (gravissima causa)

In order to impress the fact that there may be some prescriptions of law which are of such a nature that an ordinary grave cause will not suffice, the legislator stipulates that a most grave cause is required to obtain its relaxation or to grant a permission contrary to the law. Thus, even after a dispensation from the impediment of mixed religion has been obtained, the legislator forbids the parties to present themselves before a non-Catholic minister, in the exercise of his power as minister, in order to give or to renew their matrimonial consent, whether this be done before or after the Catholic ceremony.[54] That this prohibition imposes a most grave obligation is apparent from the penalty inflicted on those who act contrary to this statute. The Catholic who would transgress this law incurs an excommunication reserved to the ordinary,[55] because the appearance before a non-Catholic minister under such circumstances would constitute an active participation *in sacris* with heretics and schismatics.[56]

It is not surprising, then, that the legislator will not permit the pastor to officiate at a marriage should the pastor certainly know that the parties concerned will violate or have already

[54] Canon 1063, § 1.

[55] Canon 2319, § 1, n. 1.

[56] Canon 1258, § 1.

violated this law, unless a most grave cause is present, all danger of scandal is removed, and the ordinary is consulted.[57] The cause which will permit the pastor to officiate at the aforesaid marriage will necessarily have to be in proportion to the gravity of the prohibition and the scandal which will possibly result. The legislator does not indicate which particular cause can be considered as most grave. The authors, however, agree that, if it is foreseen that the contractants will otherwise enter into an invalid marriage by presenting themselves only before the non-Catholic minister and will neglect a Catholic marriage altogether as a result of the refusal to assist at their marriage and that as a result the religious education of the children will be entirely neglected, this is to be considered as a most grave cause which is in proportion to the law, especially if the *cautiones* have already been given.[58]

### *Section G. Most grave and most urgent cause* (gravissima et urgentissima causa)

Still another gradation of a grave cause is the "most grave and most urgent cause". The Code of Canon Law stipulates that only for a most grave and most urgent cause may the bishop permit a marriage of conscience.[59] The gravity of this law is manifest by the fact that this is the only instance in the entire Code of Canon Law that such a cause is demanded for a permission or a dispensation. Furthermore, such a marriage, since it is a secret one brings about many and great hardships to the spouses, to their children and to others as well.[60] The spouses would have to endure hardships because, more often than not, they would be unable to lead a common conjugal life even though they had the right to the use of marriage provided scandal was removed. Then, too, there is the danger of polygamy, for the husband could rather easily

57 Canon 1063, § 2.

58 Cf. Gasparri, *De Matrimonio,* I, n. 460; Cappello, *De Sacramentis,* V, n. 317; Wernz-Vidal, *Ius Canonicum,* V, n. 182; Chelodi, *De Matrimonio,* n. 61.

59 Canon 1104.

60 Cf. Payen, *De Matrimonio,* II, n. 1939.

desert his lawful wife whom he married secretly and contract another marriage invalidly with another woman.[61]

The children would be subject to many hardships. They could readily be deserted by their parents, their baptism and their education woefully and completely neglected. Even if they should be properly reared, there would still be the ever present danger that they might be considered as illegitimate and might suffer the loss of the benefits which are properly theirs as legitimate heirs.[62]

Society as a whole would also suffer because the spouses, should they live in intimate familiarity, will give occasion to grave scandal and will be accused of illicit cohabitation by those who are unaware of the secret marriage. Because of the possibility of these great hardships and evils, as well as the grave scandal that could result from a marriage of conscience, it is little wonder that the Church is reluctant to permit a marriage of conscience unless most grave and most urgent causes are present. The very nature of marriage calls for a public celebration as well as public recognition of marriage. Furthermore, it is contrary to the spirit of the law to permit secret marriages and allow them to remain occult for long.[63]

Before proceeding to the examination of the causes which could be deemed as most grave and thus sufficient and in proportion to the gravity of the law forbidding marriages of conscience, it must be noted that utmost urgency or necessity must be simultaneously present. The celebration of such a marriage must be necessary to avoid spiritual and temporal hardships which would befall the spouses or their children, and the only possible way to avoid such a state of affairs must be by a secret marriage. A mere desire of the contractants to keep their marriage a secret from friends and relatives in order to surprise them at a later date is definitely not a cause for which a permission to enter a marriage of con-

[61] Cf. Benedictus XIV, ep. encycl., *Satis Vobis,* 17 nov. 1741, § 2 — *Fontes,* n. 319.

[62] Cf., *Ibid.,* § 3 — *Fontes,* n. 319.

[63] Cf. Wernz-Vidal, *Ius Canonicum,* V, n. 566.

science could be granted. Neither will the ordinary causes which are deemed sufficient for some dispensations from matrimonial impediments or from the publication of banns be acceptable as sufficiently grave. The fact that a young woman has attained the age in which her prospects of marriage are limited, or that she comes from a very small town where marriage prospects are slim, cannot be accepted as most grave and most urgent causes.[64]

Since the Code of Canon Law does not indicate which cause is to be considered as most grave and most urgent, it must be ascertained from the practice of the Roman Curia. The Sacred Penitentiary was wont to grant this permission to a man and woman living together as husband and wife, and accepted as such by the general public, even though in reality they lived in concubinage, since it would expose them to great hardships and derision should they be required to marry in public and have the marriage banns published.[65]

A most grave cause is adjudged to be present if the marriage is necessary for the pursuit of a greater good, as for example, when the couple cannot fulfill the civil requirements because of a previous invalid civil marriage of one of the parties from which a civil divorce cannot be obtained. At the same time the only remedy for the illicit situation lies in a Catholic marriage, in order to safeguard the spiritual welfare and the salvation of the parties. Such a marriage of necessity must be kept a secret;[66] and similar to this is the case of a nobleman who desires to marry a woman not of a noble family, or from an obscure family, after he has illicitly fathered her children, but who endeavors to avoid the dis-

[64] Cf. Coburn, *Marriages of Conscience,* The Catholic University of America Canon Law Studies, n. 191 (Washington, D. C.: The Catholic University of America Press, 1944), p. 76.

[65] Cf. Benedictus XIV, ep. encycl. *Satis Vobis,* § 6—*Fontes,* n. 319.

[66] Cf. Vlaming, *Praelectiones Iuris Matrimonii ad Normam Iuris Canonici* (3. ed., 2 vols., Brussum in Hollandia: Sumptibus Editricis Anonymae, olim Paulus Brand, 1919-1921), II, n. 593; Vermeersch-Creusen, *Epitome Iuris Canonici,* II, n. 410.

approval of his family and possible disinheritance, as well as malicious derision.[67]

In any event it is left to the prudent judgment of the ordinary of the place, to the exclusion of the vicar general,[68] to determine when the circumstances are such that a marriage of conscience can be permitted. The Ordinary decides when the necessary proportion exists between the motives and the law, the gravity of each being weighed in the balance, and only then can the prescriptions of canon 84, § 1 be satisfied.

### Article 3. Necessity of a Cause

Ecclesiastical law, like all law, is a regulation in accordance with reason, enacted for the common welfare of the members of the Church. This regulation must be observed by all the members of the Church community, for otherwise, the common good will suffer harm. There may be instances, however, wherein this regulation may have to be relaxed. Naturally, this should be done only for a good reason, otherwise the one to whom the administration is entrusted would be guilty of trespassing the principles of distributive justice. He would rightfully be accused of showing undue partiality to the certain few who would thus be freed from the observance of the law. To forestall any such eventuality the Code of Canon Law has decreed in canon 84, § 1, that a dispensation from the law is to be granted only for a just and reasonable cause. Since the scope of this work envisions only dispensations granted by a subordinate dispensing agent, the necessity of the cause as affecting the validity of such a dispensation will alone be considered.

#### *Section A. Effect of lack of a cause*

A dispensation from the law of a Superior granted by a subordinate dispensing agent is both unlawful and invalid, if

[67] Cf. Wernz-Vidal, *Ius Canonicum,* V, n. 567; Payen, *De Matrimonio,* II, n. 1941; Vlaming, *op. cit.,* II, n. 593; De Smet, *De Sponsalibus et Matrimonio,* n. 160.

[68] Canon 1104.

this is done without a just and reasonable cause.[69] The subordinate dispensing agent can act only in virtue of the delegation by the Superior, or by vicarious ordinary power, in other words, he acts in the name of another: this faculty to dispense is granted either directly or indirectly by the legislator. Should the subordinate dispensing agent use this faculty and grant a dispensation without a cause, his action would definitely be an abuse of his powers and consequently his act would be invalid. It would be entirely irrational to presume that a Superior would grant his delegate the power to perform unreasonable acts; and yet that is exactly what would ensue should a subordinate dispensing agent have the faculty to grant dispensations without a cause. The Superior legislator does not grant powers to dispense from his laws indiscriminately, nor to grant dispensations rashly and unjustly; the faculty to dispense is conceded only to be exercised reasonably and prudently, presupposing the existence of a sufficient cause.[70] Should a delegate dare to abuse the faculty to dispense by granting a dispensation without a cause, his action would exceed his mandate and the dispensation would be null and void.[71]

The invalidity of a dispensation by a subordinate dispensing authority results not only from the lack of a cause, but also whenever the proposed cause is certainly insufficient for the dispensation which is sought. The cause for a dispensation

69 Canon 84, § 1.

70 Cf. Salmanticenses, *Cursus Theologiae Moralis* (6 vols., Venetiis: apud Nicolaum Pezzana, 1714-1728), Tract, XI, c. 5, n. 70; Suarez, *De Legibus,* Lib. VI, c. 18, n. 1—Opera Omnia, VI, p. 82; Laymann, *Theologia Moralis* (ed. nova, Venetiis, 1630), Lib. I, tract. IV, c. 22, n. 11; De Justis, *De Dispensationibus Matrimonialibus,* Lib. III, c. 1, n. 20-23; Reiffenstuel, *Theologia Moralis,* tract. II, dist. IV, n. 21; Benedictus XIV, *De Synodo Dioecesana,* Lib. XIII, c. V, n. 7; D'Annibale, *Summula Theologiae Moralis* (3. ed., 3 vols., Romae: apud S. C. de Prop. Fide, 1891-1892), I, n. 233; Michiels, *Normae Generales,* II, 739; S.R.R., *Antiochem Maronitarum,* Nullitatis matrimonii 21 mart. 1935, Decisio XVII, n. 21, Coram R.P.D. Guillelmo Heard—*S.R.R. Decisiones,* XXVII (1935), 152.

71 Canon 203, § 1: "Delegatus qui sive circa res sive circa personas mandati sui fines excedit, nihil agit."

must be reasonable and just, and in due proportion to the gravity of the law.[72] Should the dispensing agent decide that the alleged cause is not in proportion to the law, then he cannot validly grant the dispensation for the cause would most certainly be insufficient. An example may show this more clearly. A Catholic man desires to contract marriage with a non-Catholic woman, who, let us assume, is thirty years old. The only cause alleged in the petition is *aetas superadulta;* this is a true cause. It is not, however, a sufficient cause since it concerns the non-Catholic party to whom a dispensation is not granted; the dispensation is granted to the Catholic party and for his benefit.[73]

The same may be said concerning a petition for a dispensation from the impediment of consanguinity in the second degree of the collateral line touching the first, and the only cause alleged—consequently, the only motivating cause—is the lack of a sufficient dowry. If it is assumed that the case is not an urgent one which would permit the use of faculties granted by Canons 1043 or 1045, the alleged cause, although a true one and a canonical one, is neither a just cause nor is it proportionate to the gravity of the prohibition of such marriages. It is certainly an insufficient cause since it was declared as such by the Sacred Congregation of the Sacraments.[74] If then, the alleged cause is certainly non-existent or is certainly insufficient, the dispensing agent would act invalidly should he grant a dispensation under such conditions.[75]

It would hardly seem probable that a dispensing agent who can dispense validly only with a just cause in proportion to the gravity of the law would be in such bad faith so as to abuse his powers to the extent of granting dispensations when he certainly knows that the cause does not exist, or if it does exist, that it is certainly insufficient for the particular dispen-

72 Canon 84, § 1.

73 Cf. Wernz-Vidal, *Ius Canonicum,* V, n. 273, p. 340; Chelodi, *De Matrimonio,* n. 59, p. 69; Cappello, *Summa Iuris Canonici,* I, n. 143, p. 152.

74 Cf. instr., 1 aug. 1931—*AAS,* XXIII (1931), 414-415.

75 Cf. Michiels, *Normae Generales,* II, 747-748.

sation which is sought. No dispensing agent possessing delegated powers or vicarious proper powers would expose his acts to certain invalidity by presuming to grant dispensations without a cause.

### *Section B. Effect of erroneous judgment of the dispensing agent*

Whereas it is the common teaching of authors that a dispensation granted by a subordinate dispensing agent without a just and reasonable cause is illicit and invalid when there is certainty concerning the objective lack of the alleged cause, there exists a great controversy concerning the validity of a dispensation when the dispensing agent, in good faith but erroneously, believed the cause was in existence but it was later found to be either non-existent or, in fact, insufficient. The authors adhere to various opinions concerning the validity of such dispensations when granted by a subordinate dispensing agent. Some claim that because of the good faith of the petitioner and the grantor, in virtue of the presumptive will of the legislator, the dispensation thus conceded would be valid at the time of concession and would remain valid even after the error has been detected. This is necessary, they claim, to obviate scruples and to allow the consciences of the grantor and the grantee to remain undisturbed.[76]

Others propound the doctrine that from the moment the error is detected the acts performed in virtue of the dispensation are invalid although acts performed before the discovery of the error are valid. This obtains for dispensations which concern many successive acts which are performed in virtue of one dispensation, e.g., dispensation from the law of fasting during Lent. The acts subsequent to the detection of the error are invalid due to the prescription of canon 86, which states that dispensations which have recurrent application cease to obtain with the cessation of the reason for which they were granted.[77] Still others hold that a dispensation granted

[76] Cf. Michiels, *Normae Generales,* II, 753; Salmanticenses, *Cursus Theologiae Moralis,* tract. XI, c. 5, n. 71.

[77] Cf. Van Hove, *De Privilegiis; De Dispensationibus,* n. 479.

for motives which were erroneously believed to exist but in fact did not, is invalid from the very beginning and all acts performed in virtue of this dispensation are invalid.[78]

The opinion which considers a dispensation granted by one who has delegated or vicarious powers to be invalid *ab initio* if the alleged motivating cause is found to be non-existent, seems to be the opinion in closer harmony with the prescription of canon 84, § 1. At first glance, this opinion may appear to be excessively strict and as placing too great a burden upon the dispensing agent who would thus be influenced to desist from granting any dispensations due to his fears lest he grant invalid dispensations. Any such fears will rather lead the grantor of dispensations to exercise greater care in considering the alleged causes. If he exerts prudent care in granting dispensations his conscience need not be unduly disturbed because from the moral standpoint his conscience will be guiltless. The presumption always favors the validity of the act, and unless proofs are presented which would overpower this presumption, the validity of the dispensation will prevail. Once the proofs are offered which will definitely show that the alleged cause was not verified in fact, that it had no objective existence at the time the dispensation was granted, then the presumption fails and the invalidity of the dispensation is established. All acts performed in view of this dispensation are invalid. If the dispensation was granted for one act, e.g., to contract marriage, then that act is invalid, except in a case wherein the law stipulates that even should there be no cause, whether it be non-existent or false, the validity of the act is not nullified.[79]

[78] Cf. Bonacina, *Opera Omnia* (3 vols., Parisiis: Joannes Branchu, 1632), T. II, disp. I, q. 2, punct. 3, n. 8; Castro-Palao, *Opus Morale,* (7 vols., Lugduni, 1700), tract. III, disp. 6, punct. 8, § 2, n. 5; D'Annibale, *Summula Theologiae Moralis,* I, n. 233; St. Adolphus, *Theologia Moralis,* Lib. III, n. 251; Ojetti, *Commentarium in Codicem Iuris Canonici,* Vol. I (Romae: Apud Aedes Universitatis Gregorianae, 1927), p. 336; Cicognani-Staffa, II, 624-625; O'Mara, *Canonical Causes for Matrimonial Dispensations,* pp. 61-63; Romani, *Institutiones Juris Canonici,* Vol. I, *Jus Constitutionale* (Romae: Apud Auctorem, 1941), I, n. 213; Rodrigo, *De Legibus,* n. 496, ad 4b.

[79] Cf. Canons 1054 and 1042, § 2.

The presumption in favor of the validity of a dispensation is not unlike the presumption granted by law to every marriage, and yet the law permits the validity of the marriage to be impugned. If the proofs are sufficient to show with moral certitude that the presumption of the law cannot be upheld, the marriage is declared null and void. The right to attack the validity of a marriage does not differ from the right to attack the validity of a dispensation; and if the Church declares a marriage null and void when a canonical irregularity of a nullifying nature is present, the same obtains for a declaration of nullity of a dispensation if the necessary cause did not exist at the time it was granted.

The opponents of this opinion would lead one to believe that it gives rise to many scruples and disturbs the conscience of those who receive the dispensation. It would leave them in a disturbed state of mind, always questioning the validity of their dispensation. This does not seem to be a valid argument because the same may be said of every marriage that is contracted. The faithful are aware of the fact that invalid marriages are possible for a good many reasons, but this fact in no way deters them from entering marriage nor does it disturb their consciences or peace of mind. There is always the possibility that there could probably be simulation of consent, or that there was a condition *contra bonum prolis* or *contra bonum sacramenti,* but this possibility does not give rise to scruples nor does it disturb the consciences of the consorts. They do not question the validity of their marriage, nor do they disturb themselves with questions whether perhaps they may have unwittingly inserted some condition or in some other way vitiated their consent. Since they were in good faith they do not trouble themselves with the thought that perhaps their marriage is null. In like manner, those who receive a dispensation in good faith do not disturb themselves with questions concerning the possible invalidity of the dispensation due to the non-existence of the cause, provided that they did not falsify the cause knowingly.

The dispensing agent, also need not be unduly disturbed, for if he acted in good faith, his act is presumed to be valid until proven otherwise. And even should the proofs definitely establish the fact that the dispensation was actually invalid due to his erroneous judgment, he is still guiltless provided he used prudent care. As long as the petitioner and the grantor were in good faith their consciences need not be disturbed, because they are free from moral guilt. The good faith, however, does not render invalid acts valid, for if this were true, then only bad faith would have a vitiating effect upon human acts. Thus if two first cousins contracted marriage unaware of the fact that they were so closely related, or unaware of the fact that a dispensation was necessary, even if they were in good faith, the marriage is definitely invalid.[80] But those who uphold validity of a dispensation because of the good faith because of the desire to leave consciences undisturbed would logically have to assert the validity of such a marriage, which is impossible.[81]

Another argument advanced by the proponents of the opinion favoring the validity of a dispensation under the conditions herein considered, is the presumed will of the legislator.[82] They base their stand on the fact that the legislator by his silence condones such a course of action. However, the commonly accepted opinion states that it cannot be presumed that a legislator would permit a dispensation without a cause.[83] The reasoning of the proponents for validity of the dispensation can logically be extended to a case wherein the motivating cause did not exist, even though the subordinate dispensing agent believed erroneously that the cause existed in reality. If it cannot be presumed that a legislator permits

[80] Canon 1076, § 2.

[81] Cf. Castro-Palao, *Opus Morale,* tract. III, disp. 6, punct. 8, § 2, n. 5: ". . . ad rectam gubernationem Ecclesiae non pertinet firmare dispensationem sine causa, sed illas excusare: alias pertinet etiam ad rectam gubernationem ut quoties dispensandi putarent bona fide nullam sibi dispensationem esse necessariam, validos actus efficerent, nulla adhibita dispensatione, sic contrahentes bona fide in gradibus prohibitis valide contraherent, quod non est admittendum."

[82] Cf. Michiels, *Normae Generales,* II, 751.

[83] Cf. De Justis, *De Dispensationibus Matrimonialibus,* Lib. II, c. 2, n. 49; Schmalzgrueber, *Jus Ecclesiasticum Universum,* Lib. IV, tit. 16, § 5, n. 147.

a delegate to dispense without a cause but that such a power must be explicitly granted in the faculties conceded to him, it means that the delegate will exceed the mandate should the motivating cause be non-existent, and his action is invalid. Furthermore, a cause which is adjudged erroneously to exist when actually it does not, is the same as if there were no cause at all; consequently a dispensation granted under such circumstances is invalid. Even should some cause be alleged in good faith by the petitioner but in reality it did not exist, it basically becomes a false cause, and a false cause is no cause at all.

Michiels, perhaps the most staunch advocate of the validity of a dispensation after subsequent discovery of the error concerning the existence of the alleged cause, admits that in theory there is no doubt that in virtue of canon 84, § 1 such a dispensation is invalid from the time it is granted. This is true because objectively no just cause is present whereas the validity of the dispensation depends not upon the subjective estimation of the dispensing agent but on the objective existence of the cause.[84] He admits, then, that the intrinsic and legal arguments militate against the validity of a dispensation thus granted. In practice, however, he would reject the intrinsic arguments for extrinsic authority. He claims instead that such dispensations should be considered valid due to the many authors who adhered to this doctrine before the promulgation of the Code of Canon Law. He calls upon the pre-Code interpretation to explain the present law, which, he claims, is based upon the pre-Code legislation.[85] Even if this were verified in fact,[86] there were other very serious authors[87]

[84] Cf. *Normae Generales,* II, 752.

[85] *Loc. cit.*

[86] O'Mara (*Canonical Causes for Matrimonial Dispensations,* pp. 62-63) very effectively shows how the misinterpretation of the doctrine of Sanchez and Schmalzgrueber has led Michiels in his first edition (1929) of *Normae Generales,* II, 510 to an erroneous conclusion; he adheres to the same theory in his second edition, II, 752; cf. also S.R.R. *Varsavien* Nullitatis matrimonii, 6 maii 1926, Decision XXI, n. 3, coram R.P.D. Josepho Florczak — *S.R.R. Decisiones,* XVIII (1926), 169.

[87] E.g., Sanchez, *De Sancto Matrimonii Sacramento,* Lib. III, disp. 5, n. 6; St. Alphonsus, *Theologia Moralis,* Lib. VI, n. 990.

in the pre-Code era who held the very opposite opinion and the controversy existed even then. It is difficult, then, on these grounds to uphold the theory which propounds the validity of such dispensations since the arguments are based only on extrinsic rather than intrinsic authority.

Consequently, a dispensation which is granted for a cause whose non-existence is subsequently proven, although it be sought and granted in good faith, must be considered as invalid *ab initio,* if the tenets of canon 84, § 1, are to be preserved. It may appear that in practice many hardships may result from the literal interpretation and rigorous application of this canon. There are, however, practical solutions for the cases wherein the dispensation is found to be invalid due to the discovery of the absence of a motivating cause. If the dispensation has recurrent application then once the non-existence of a just cause is detected, no further use of the dispensation is possible, but a new petition must be made to the dispensing authority presenting just and reasonable causes. If the dispensation is not for recurrent application but was for one solitary act which once performed is not repeated, as a dispensation from a matrimonial impediment, proper remedies are applicable. If the dispensation was for a minor impediment,[88] then no one need be troubled since the marriage is valid.[89] If the dispensation is for a major diriment impediment, the marriage is to be considered as invalid. In such cases, the parties need not be forced to discontinue their common life since this would cause great inconvenience especially if there were any children. Then, too, it might cause scandal since the couple as well as all the neighbors believed that the marriage was valid. In such cases the parties concerned need not even be told of the invalidity if it is prudently foreseen that scandal may result, but the *sanatio in radice* can be applied. If however, the parties were aware of the invalidity of the dispensation, then a new dispensation can be granted and a convalidation of the marriage can follow. This course of

88 Canon 1042, § 2.

89 Canon 1054.

action would be parallel to a case wherein a couple contracted marriage before a pastor who assisted at a marriage after erroneously petitioning for and receiving a dispensation from mixed religion whereas a dispensation from disparity of cult was necessary. Such a marriage is invalid but in practice the marriage is validated by application of the *sanatio in radice,* leaving the consciences of the parties undisturbed. If on the other hand, the parties have separated or perhaps have even received a civil decree of divorce, showing they no longer desire to lead a common conjugal life, they may petition for a declaration of nullity on the grounds of an invalid dispensation.[90] Once the petition is presented to the Tribunal a formal process will have to be instituted during which it will have to be proven that the motivating cause alleged in the petition for the dispensation did not exist at the time the dispensation was granted.

When the error in the judgment of the dispensing authority concerns the sufficiency of the cause, that is, whether the cause was sufficiently just and reasonable, a distinction must be made. If the existing cause is shown to be certainly unjust and unreasonable, lacking the due proportion to the law from which the dispensation was granted, the dispensation is invalid for the same reasons as explained in the preceding arguments concerning the erroneous estimation concerning the existence of a cause.[91] If there is a doubt as to the sufficiency of the alleged motivating cause which nonetheless exists objectively, the dispensation is considered as valid under the tenets of canon 84, § 2.

When the dispensing authority erroneously believes that the alleged motivating cause does not exist, but *de facto* it does exist, and the dispensation is nonetheless granted, it is valid. This appears to be a purely academic problem because it

90 Cf. O'Mara, *Canonical Causes for Matrimonial Dispensations,* p. 63.

91 Cf. Bonacina, *Opera Omnia,* Tom. II, disp. I, q. 2, punct. 3, n. 8: "Bona fides petentis dispensationem sine causa non efficit dispensationem validam; ergo nec illam reddit validam bona fides concedentis, qui bona fide putabat legitimam et sufficientem causam subesse, quamvis bona fides utrumque excuset a peccato donec de insufficientia causae constiterit."

seems to be most improbable that a dispensing authority would grant dispensations under these conditions. Such a dispensation would be illicit since the grantor would have the intention of acting contrary to the law as prescribed by canon 84, § 1. It would nevertheless be valid because the validity of the dispensation is determined from the objective existence of the cause and not from the subjective estimation of the dispensing authority.[92]

### *Section C. Doubt concerning the existence of a cause*

There are some authors who can see no difference between the doubtful insufficiency of a cause and the doubtful existence of a sufficient cause.[93] Considering the two concepts objectively, it is quite apparent that there is a difference between the two. The doubtful insufficiency of a cause presupposes its very existence; the doubt concerns only whether this existing cause can be considered as a sufficient motivating cause for this particular dispensation. In the second case, the doubt concerns the very existence of the cause, the insufficiency of which cannot be the object of a judgment unless its existence is first established. Canon 84, § 2 governs the valid granting of dispensations when there is doubt concerning the sufficiency of the proposed motivating cause; it does not, however, validate the dispensation when there is a doubt whether the cause exists at all.[94] If there is a doubt concerning the existence of a motivating cause, the principles enumerated in canon 84, § 1 must be applied, and if the doubt cannot be resolved, no dispensation may be granted by the subordinate dispensing

[92] Cf. Sanchez, *De Sancto Matrimonii Sacramento,* Lib. VIII, disp. 17, n. 11; St. Alphonsus, *Theologia Moralis,* Lib. I, n. 181; Michiels, *Normae Generales,* II, 750; O'Mara, *Canonical Causes for Matrimonial Dispensations,* p. 64; Rodrigo, *De Legibus,* n. 491.

[93] Cf. Michiels, *Normae Generales,* II, 754; Coronata, *Institutiones Iuris Canonici,* I, n. 115; Rodrigo, *De Legibus,* n. 490, n. 3.

[94] Cf. Vermeersch-Creusen, *Epitome Iuris Canonici,* I, n. 197; Vromant, *Facultates Apostolicae* (3 ed., Parisiis: Desclee de Brouwer, 1947), n. 61; Van Hove, *De Privilegiis; De Dispensationibus,* n. 477; De Smet, *De Sponsalibus et Matrimonio,* n. 812.

agent. There is no canon which could be invoked whereby the doubtfully existent cause could assume the stature of a sufficient cause.[95]

Some, by resolving the doubtful existence of the motivating cause into a doubt of fact, would concede the dispensing agent the faculty to grant a valid dispensation in virtue of canon 15.[96] This canon stipulates that in a doubt of fact the ordinary can dispense from invalidating and disqualifying laws from which the Supreme Pontiff is wont to dispense. Canon 15 deals primarily with a case in which the doubt concerns the need of a dispensation and merely gives the ordinary the faculty to grant the needed dispensation if the law is one from which the Pope usually dispenses.[97] It does not envision the case in which a dispensation is certainly necessary but the doubt concerns the existence of the cause in virtue of which the dispensation may be granted. The doubtful existence of the cause is not a doubt of the fact but rather a doubt of the necessary motive which is an essential element whenever a dispensation is granted by a subordinate dispensing authority.

Others, because of the probable existence of the motivating cause, assert the validity of the dispensation in virtue of canon 209, claiming the necessary jurisdiction is supplied by the Church in a positive and probable doubt of fact. The basis for this opinion seems to be that the ordinary has probable faculties to dispense validly in such instances.[98] But canon 209 does not grant unlimited faculties to relax the common law, and it has been shown that the faculty to dispense without a cause cannot be presumed.[99] There is no doubt that the faculties of subordinate dispensing authorities extend only to those cases in which a just and reasonable cause is actually

[95] Cf. O'Mara, *Canonical Causes for Matrimonial Dispensations*, p. 65.

[96] Cf. Cappello, *Summa Iuris Canonici*, I, n. 133; Reilly, *The General Norms of Dispensation*, p. 114; Uribe, *De Episcoporum Ordinaria Dispensandi Facultate* (Medelii in Colombia: Typographia Bedout, 1939), n. 144.

[97] Cf. Van Hove, *De Privilegiis; De Dispensationibus*, n. 477, p. 438; Cappiello, *De Ordinariorum Dispensandi Facultate ad Normam Can. 81*, pp. 84-85.

[98] Cf. Michiels, *Normae Generales*, II, 754.

[99] Cf. supra p. 84.

present.[100] Canon 209 supplies jurisdiction in a positive and probable doubt when it is not otherwise present. Now in canon 84, § 1, the dispensing authority is certainly given jurisdiction, so there is no question as to his faculty to dispense under the specified conditions. Thus the prescription of canon 209 cannot supply the cause for a dispensation when it does not exist, it supplies only jurisdiction; a dispensation which is invalid due to a lack of a cause cannot, even *post factum,* be validated in virtue of canon 209.

### *Section D. Effect of subreption and obreption*

The normal procedure in granting a dispensation is through the use of a rescript: consequently the vices which militate against the validity of a rescript will have the same effect upon a dispensation, which is granted in view of the petition addressed to the one in authority. The petition must be formulated in the accepted way and the reasons alleged must be truthfully presented. If the petitioner conceals the truth (subreption) which is not considered as essential by the Roman Curia, but fulfills the other requirements of the law, the dispensation is valid.[101] If however the petitioner conceals those facts which the Curial practice demands as necessary, then even if this was done in good faith, through ignorance or inadvertence, the dispensation would be invalid.[102] Thus, for example, if a dispensation was refused by the vicar general, and this refusal is not mentioned in the petition to the ordinary, even should the ordinary grant the dispensation it would be invalid.[103]

The effect of obreption is of greater practical importance in regard to the purview herein considered. Obreption, or falsification of the cause, will have greater bearing on the validity or invalidity of the dispensation whether it be granted by the subordinate dispensing authority or by the legislator himself.

100 Canon 84, § 1.

101 Canon 42, § 1.

102 Cf. Michiels, *Normae Generales,* II, 361-363; Van Hove, *De Rescriptis,* n. 155.

103 Canon 44, § 2.

Obreption must be considered objectively, so that if the alleged cause does not correspond to the truth, it will vitiate the dispensation whatever the cause of the obreption may be. Good or bad faith in obreption is indifferent: it matters little whether the cause is falsified in good faith, bad faith, error, ignorance, fraud or malice, the dispensation will nonetheless be invalid, if the one and only alleged cause is false.[104] If obreption is practiced in the petition, some distinctions must be made before it can be determined whether the dispensation is valid or not. First of all, it must be understood that the petition must conform with canon 40: the prescription *si preces veritate nitantur* must be observed for dispensations as well as for rescripts.

The petition for a dispensation may list either one solitary cause or it may list many causes. If only one cause is alleged, it is presumed to be the motivating cause, and if this is falsified, the dispensation is invalid. If however more than one motivating cause is alleged, then as long as one of the causes is verified in fact, the dispensation is valid.[105] If the causes alleged are only impelling causes without a cause which could be adjudged as motivating, all of these causes taken together could constitute one motive cause;[106] but if one of these is false, the dispensation is invalid, unless the number of impelling causes alleged is in such great number that, even if one were false, the others being truthful, will still have the effect of a true motive cause.[107]

In this entire treatise on false or falsified causes, it must be borne in mind that if the dispensation is from a minor matrimonial impediment, neither subreption nor obreption invali-

[104] Cf. Cappello, *Summa Iuris Canonici,* I, n. 150; Van Hove, *De Rescriptis,* n. 156; Michiels, *Normae Generales,* II, 371; Cicognani-Staffa, pp. 341 and 349.

[105] Canon 42, § 2.

[106] Cf. S. C. de Prop. Fide, instr., 9 maii 1877 — *Collectanea S. C. de Prop. Fide,* n. 1470; *Fontes,* n. 4890.

[107] Cf. Cappello, *Summa Iuris Canonici,* I, n. 152, ad 5; Van Hove, *De Rescriptis,* n. 159; Michiels, *Normae Generales,* II, 367; Cicognani-Staffa, II, 347.

date it whether falsification was in good or bad faith.[108] If the falsification is made in bad faith, the dispensation is illicit, and the petitioner is morally guilty. Furthermore, such moral guilt may be punished by the bishop.[109]

### Article 4. Examination of the Alleged Cause

It is the common teaching of present day authors, that the examination and knowledge of the alleged cause for a dispensation is not required for validity.[110] Even though the examination of the cause is not required for validity, it is nevertheless required for its lawfulness. Consequently it is the moral obligation of the dispensing agent to verify the actual existence, the truthfulness and sufficiency of the cause lest the dispensation be exposed to invalidity.

All who are in any way connected with the dispensation, whether it be with the petition or with the actual grant, are under the obligation to ascertain that the alleged cause is objectively truthful. The petitioner should be made to realize that he is bound by the grave moral obligation to advance only truthful and existing causes when a petition is made for a dispensation. All too often the faithful are given the impression that the required causes in a petition are a mere formality: a technicality which has no meaning. Ordinarily the faithful come to their pastor or to some other priest of the parish and forward the petition for a dispensation through them to the bishop. The duty to ascertain that the alleged causes are verified in fact, devolves upon the priest because the dispensing authority cannot be expected to examine personally each and every cause as alleged by the petitioner. It is physically impossible for the bishop to have knowledge of every cause or to examine each cause in the petitions for dis-

108 Cf. canons 1054 and 1042, § 2.

109 Canon 2361.

110 Cf. Van Hove, *De Privilegiis; De Dispensationibus,* n. 472; Michiels, *Normae Generales,* II, 747; Cicognani-Staffa, II, 621; Rodrigo, *De Legibus,* n. 491; Wernz-Vidal, *Ius Canonicum,* I, n. 318; O'Mara, *Canonical Causes for Matrimonial Dispensations,* p. 59; Reilly, *General Norms of Dispensations,* p. 117; Coronata, *Institutiones Iuris Canonici,* I, n. 115, 2.

pensations; his obligation is not necessarily a personal one, and it can be delegated: this is the practice generally followed. This is analogous to the forwarding of petitions for dispensations by the bishop to the Holy See.

It often happens that the actual petitioner for a dispensation is not aware that a special reason is needed for a dispensation and is not prepared to give a cause. The priest who makes the petition in the name of one of the parishioners, is obliged to ascertain whether there actually is a motive cause which is just and reasonable; this can be done by prudent questioning. He is not at liberty to tell the petitioners that he will see to it that a dispensation is secured and then proceed to enter a cause from the list of accepted canonical causes, without the knowledge whether the cause exists in the particular case at hand. Such procedure is practiced at times, unfortunately, in petitioning for a dispensation for a marriage. It has become altogether too general a practice to presuppose that because a Catholic wishes to marry a non-Catholic, there is a universal danger of a marriage outside the Church. True, this may be verified in a majority of such cases, but it must be determined by prudent questioning and not taken for granted in all cases of mixed religion or disparity of cult dispensations. The priest who forwards the petition is morally bound to determine as far as he is capable whether there is a just and reasonable cause, for otherwise he is exposing the dispensing authority to the danger of acting invalidly. If the dispensation is from a minor impediment and the priest enters a cause which he has not verified, the dispensation is valid,[111] but he is still guilty of a gravely illicit action for which he can be punished. If the dispensation is from a major diriment impediment, such action on the part of the priest is gravely illicit and furthermore he renders the action of the dispensing agent invalid with the consequent invalidity of the marriage as well. Thus the obligation of the priest to ascertain the objective existence of the causes which he alleges in the petition in the name of the parishioners is quite apparent from

111 Canons 1054 and 1042, § 2.

the consequences which ensue should it be later discovered that the alleged causes were not true but were falsified either by the petitioners or by the priest himself.

Although the dispensing agent is not required to examine personally the alleged causes in a petition for a dispensation, he is not devoid of moral responsibility. The dispensing agent, whether he be the ordinary of the diocese, or whether he be the chancellor or any other official delegated by the bishop, is obliged to examine the alleged causes in order to determine whether the alleged cause is sufficient for the dispensation requested. This is true not only of matrimonial dispensations but all others as well. The practice of "rubber-stamping" each and every petition without due consideration as to the merits of the alleged causes, without weighing the gravity of the law and the danger to the common good in counterbalance to the gravity of the alleged causes but taking for granted that all the alleged causes are always sufficient, cannot be condoned because it is gravely illicit.

## CONCLUSIONS

1. The concept of "reasonable cause" adds emphasis to the concept of a "just cause"; it both states and emphasizes the fact that a proportion between the alleged cause and the gravity of the law must be determined prudently and with equity. (pp. 66-67)

2. Despite the opinion of some authors, dispensations granted for causes which were subsequently proved to be non-existent objectively are invalid, with the exception, however, of the dispensations granted in the event of matrimonial impediments of minor degree, as determined by canons 1042, § 2, and 1054. (p. 82)

3. There is no basis in Canon Law for the assertion that the presumptive will of the legislator validates a dispensation granted for causes erroneously believed to exist. (pp. 84-85)

4. The doubtful existence of a cause cannot be juridically reduced to the doubtful sufficiency of a cause indicated in canon 84, § 2. (pp. 87-88)

5. Doubt regarding the very existence of a cause is not a doubt of fact as indicated by canon 15. (pp. 88-89)

6. Canon 209 cannot be invoked for the validation of dispensations which are otherwise invalid in consequence of the objective non-existence of a sufficient cause. (pp. 89-90)

# BIBLIOGRAPHY

## Sources

*Acta Apostolicae Sedis, Commentarium Officiale,* Romae, 1909-1929; Civitate Vaticana 1929.

*Acta Sanctae Sedis,* 41 vols., Romae, 1865-1908.

*Codex Iuris Canonici Pii X Pontificis Maximi iussu digestus, Benedicti Papae XV auctoritate promulgatus,* Romae: Typis Polyglottis Vaticanis, 1917.

*Codicis Iuris Canonici Fontes,* cura Emi Petri Card. Gasparri editi (9 vols., Romae: Typis Polyglottis Vaticanis, 1923-1939. Vols. VII-IX, ed. cura et studio Emi Iustiniani Card. Serédi).

*Collectanea S. Congregationis de Propaganda Fide,* 2 vols., Romae: Typographia Polyglottis S. C. de Propaganda Fide, 1907.

*Corpus Iuris Canonici,* ed. Richter-Friedberg, 2 vols., Lipsiae, 1879-1881.

*Decretales D. Gregorii Papae IX, suae integritati una cum glossis restitutae,* Romae: in Aedibus Populi Romani, 1582.

*Decretum Gratiani, emendatum et notationibus illustratum cum glossis Gregorii XIII, Pont. Max. jussu editum,* 2 vols., Romae: in Aedibus Populi Romani, 1582.

Hardouin, J., *Acta Conciliorum et Epistolae Decretales ac Constitutiones Summorum Pontificum,* 12 vols., Parisiis, 1714-1715.

Jaffé, P., *Regesta Pontificum Romanorum ab condita Ecclesia ad annum post Christum natum MCXCVIII,* ed. 2 correctam et auctam auspiciis Gulielmi Wattenbach curaverunt S. Loewenfeld, F. Kaltenbrunner, P. Ewald, 2 vols., Lipsiae, 1885-1888.

*Liber Sextus Decretalium D. Bonifacii Papae VIII, suae integritati cum Clementinis et Extravagantibus, earumque glossis restitutis,* Romae: in Aedibus Populi Romani, 1582.

Mansi, J. P., *Sacrorum Conciliorum Nova et Amplissima Collectio,* 53 vols. in 60, Parisiis, 1901-1927.

*Monumenta Germaniae Historica, Libelli de Lite,* 3 vols., editi a G. H. Pertz, Hannoverae, 1891-1897.

Potthast, A., *Regesta Pontificum Romanorum inde ab anno post Christum natum MCXCVIII ad annum MCCCIV,* 2 vols., Berolini, 1874-1875.

*Sacrae Romanae Rotae Decisiones seu Sententiae, quae prodierunt anno 1909-* Romae: Typis Polyglottis Vaticanis, 1912-.

Schroeder, H. J., *Canons and Decrees of the Council of Trent,* St. Louis: Herder Book Co., 1950.

## Reference Works

Alphonsus M. de Ligorio, *Theologia Moralis,* ed. nova, 4 vols., cura L. Gaudé, Romae, 1905-1912.

Ballerini, A. Palmieri, D., *Opus Theologicum Morale,* 2 ed., 7 vols., Prati: Ex Officina Libraria Giachetti, Filii et Soc., 1892-1894.

Bangen, J., *Instructio Practica de Sponsalibus et Matrimonio,* 4 vols. in 1, Monasterii, 1858-1860.

Barbosa, A., *De Officio et Potestate Episcopi,* 3 vols., Lugduni, 1656.

———, *Iuris Ecclesiastici Universi Libri Tres,* Lugduni, 1650.

Benedictus XIV, *De Synodo Dioecesana,* 2 vols., Parmae, 1764.

Berutti, C., *Institutiones Iuris Canonici,* 6 vols. in 7, Taurini-Romae: Marietti, Vol. I, 1936; Vol. II, Pars I, 1943; Vol. III, 1936, Vol. IV, 1940; Vol. VI, 1938.

Boich, H., *In Quinque Decretalium Libros Commentaria,* Venetiis: apud Haeredem Hieronimi Scoti, 1576.

Bonacina, M., *Opera Omnia,* 3 vols., Parisiis: Joannes Branchu, 1632.

Bouix, D., *Tractatus de Episcopo,* 2 ed., 2 vols., Parisiis: apud Perisse fratres, 1873.

Bouquillon, T., *Theologia Moralis Fundamentalis,* 2 ed., Ratisbonae- Cinn.-Neo Eboraci: Pustet, 1890.

Brys, J., *De Dispensatione in Iure Canonico,* Brugis: Beyaert, 1925.

Cappello, F., *Summa Iuris Canonici,* 3 vols., Romae: apud Aedes Universitatis Gregorianae. Vol. I and II, 4. ed., 1945; Vol. III, 2. ed., 1940.

———, *Tractatus canonico-moralis de Sacramentis,* 5 vols., Taurini-Romae: Marietti. Vol. I, *De Sacramentis, in Genere, de Baptismo, Confirmatione et Eucharistia,* 5. ed., 1947; Vol. V, *De Matrimonio,* 6. ed., 1950.

Cappiello, L., *De Ordinariorum Dispensandi Facultate ad Normam Can. 81,* The Catholic University of America Canon Law Studies, n. 323, Washington, D. C.: The Catholic University of America Press, 1952.

Castro-Palao, F., *Opus Morale,* 7 vols., Lugduni, 1700.

Chelodi, J., *Ius Canonicum De Matrimonio,* 5. ed., a Pio Ciprotti aucta, Vincenza: Societate Anonima Typografica Editrice, 1947.

Cicognani, A., *Commentarium ad Librum I Codicis,* Romae: Ex schola Typographica "Pio X" 1925.

———, *Ius Canonicum,* Romae: Ex Officina Typographica, 1925.

Cicognani, A. Staffa, D., *Commentarium ad Librum Primum Codicis Iuris Canonici,* 2 vols., Vol. I, Romae: Ex Officina Typographica Romana "Buona Stampa", 1939; Vol. II, Romae: apud Custodiam Librariam Pontificii Instituti Utriusque Juris, 1942.

Coburn, V., *Marriage of Conscience,* The Catholic University of America Canon Law Studies, n. 191, Washington, D. C.: The Catholic University of America Press, 1944.

Coronata, M. Conte a, *Institutiones Iuris Canonici,* editio altera, 5 vols., Taurini: Marietti, 1939-1947.

D'Annibale, J., *Summula Theologiae Moralis,* 3. ed., 3 vols., Romae: apud S. C. de Propaganda Fide, 1891-1892.

De Justis, V., *Tractatus de Dispensationibus Matrimonialibus in Tres Libros Digestus,* Venetiis, 1759.

De Smet, A., *De Sponsalibus et Matrimonio,* 4. ed., Brugis: Beyaert, 1927.

De Soto, D., *De Iustitia et Iure,* Venetiis, 1568.

*Dictionnaire de Droit Canonique,* Paris: Letouzey et Ane, 1924-.

Durandus, G., *Speculum Iuris,* 4 vols. in 3, Venetiis: apud Juntas, 1577.

Esmein, A., *Le Mariage en Droit Canonique,* 2. ed., mise à jour par R. Génestal et Jean Dauvillier, 2 vols., Paris: Libr. de Recueil Sirey, 1929-1935.

Farrugia, N., *De Matrimonio et Causis Matrimonialibus,* Taurini: Marietti, 1924.

Febronius, J., (Nicholaus von Hontheim), *De Statu Ecclesiae et Legitima Postestate Romani Pontificis,* Bullioni: apud Guillelmum Evrardi, 1765.

Feiji, H., *De Impedimentis et Dispensationibus Matrimonialibus,* 3. ed., Lovanii, 1885.

Ferraris, L., *Prompta Bibliotheca Canonica, Juridica, Moralis, Theologica, necnon Ascetica, Polemica, Rubristica, Historica,* ed. novissima, 9 vols., Romae, 1885-1899.

Gasparri, P., *Tractatus Canonicus de Matrimonio,* ed. nova ad mentem Codicis Canonici, 2 vols., Romae: Typis Polyglottis Vaticinis, 1932.

Guido de Baysio, *Commentarium super Sexto Decretalium,* Venetiis, 1577.

Guiniven, J., *The Precept of Hearing Mass,* The Catholic University of America Canon Law Studies, n. 158, Washington, D. C.: The Catholic University of America Press, 1942.

Hostiensis (Henricus de Segusio), *Summa Aurea,* Venetiis, 1570.

————, *Commentaria in Quinque Decretalium Libros,* 5 vols. in 3, Venetiis, 1581.

Innocentius IV, *Commentaria in Quinque Libros Decretalium,* Venetiis, 1570.

Koudelka, C., *Pastors, Their Rights and Obligations,* The Catholic University of America Canon Law Studies, n. 11, Washington, D. C.: The Catholic University of America, 1921.

Laymann, P., *Theologia Moralis,* ed. nova, Venetiis, 1630.

Maroto, Ph., *Institutiones Iuris Canonici,* 2 vols., Romae, 1919-1921; Vol. I, 3. ed., Romae, 1921.

Michiels, G., *Normae Generales Juris Canonici,* 2. ed., 2 vols., Parisiis-Tornaci-Romae: Desclée et Socii, 1949.

Migne, L., *Patrologiae Cursus Completus,* Series Latina, 221 vols., Parisiis, 1844-1855.

Ojetti, B., *Commentarium in Codicem Iuris Canonici,* Liber I, Romae: apud Aedes Universitatis Gregorianae, 1927.

————, *Synopsis Rerum Moralium et Iuris Pontificii,* 3. ed., 4 vols., Romae, 1909-1914.

O'Keefe, G., *Matrimonial Dispensations, Power of Bishops, Priests and Confessors,* The Catholic University of America Canon Law Studies, n. 45, Washington, D. C.: The Catholic University of America, 1927.

O'Mara, W., *Canonical Causes for Matrimonial Dispensations,* The Catholic University of America Canon Law Studies, n. 96, Washington, D. C.: The Catholic University of America, 1935.

Panormitanus, Abbas (Nicholaus de Tudeschis), *Commentaria in Quinque Libros Decretalium,* 5 vols. in 7, Venetiis, 1589.

Payen, G., *De Matrimonio in Missionibus ac Potissimum in Sinis,* altera editio, 3 vols., Zi-ka-wei: Typographia T'OU-SE-WE, 1935-1936.

Pontius, B., *Tractatus de Sacramento Matrimonii,* Venetiis, 1756.

Pyrrho, C. - *Praxis Dispensationum Apostolicarum,* Neapoli, 1641.

Raymundus de Pennafort, *Summa de Poenitentia et Matrimonio,* ed. nova, Veronae, 1744.

Regatillo, E., *Institutiones Iuris Canonici,* 2 vols., Santander: Sal Terrae, 1941-1942.

Reiffenstuel, A., *Jus Canonicum Universum,* 7 vols., Parisiis: apud L. Vivès, 1864-1870.

———, *Theologia Moralis,* 7. ed., 2 vols., Mutinae, 1745.

Reilly, E., *The General Norms of Dispensations,* The Catholic University of America Canon Law Studies, n. 119, Washington, D. C.: The Catholic University of America Press, 1939.

Reilly, P., *Residence of Pastors,* The Catholic University of America Canon Law Studies, n. 97, Washington, D. C.: The Catholic University of America, 1935.

Rodrigo, L., *Theologia Moralis Fundamentalis,* T. II, *Tractatus de Legibus,* Santander: Sal Terrae, 1944.

Roelker, E., *Principles of Privilege According to the Code of Canon Law,* The Catholic University of America Canon Law Studies, n. 35, Washington, D. C.: The Catholic University of America, 1926.

Romani, S., *Institutiones Juris Canonici,* Vol. I, *Jus Constitutionale,* Romae: Apud Auctorem, 1941.

Rufinus, *Die Summa Decretorum des Magister Rufinus,* ed. H. Singer, Paderborn, 1902.

Salmanticenses, *Cursus Theologiae Moralis,* 6 vols., Venetiis: apud Nicolaum Pezzana, 1714-1728.

Sanchez, T., *De Sancto Matrimonii Sacramento,* 3 vols. in 1, Venetiis, 1726.

Sandeus, F., *Commentaria in Quinque Libros Decretalium,* 2 vols., Venetiis, 1570.

Schenk, F., *Matrimonial Impediment of Mixed Religion and Disparity of Cult,* The Catholic University of America Canon Law Studies, n. 51, Washington, D. C.: The Catholic University of America, 1929.

Schmalzgrueber, F., *Ius Ecclesiasticum Universum,* 5 vols. in 12, Romae, 1843-1845.

Stiegler, M. A., *Dispensation, Dispensationswesen, und Dispensationsrecht im Kirchenrecht,* Mainz, 1901.

Suarez, F., *Opera Omnia,* ed. nova a Carolo Berton, 26 vols. in 28, Parisiis: apud L. Vivès, 1856-1861. Vols. V-VI, *Tractatus de Legibus ac Deo Legislatore;* Vol. XIV, *De Voto.*

Thomas Aquinas, *Summa Theologica,* 6 vols., Parisiis, 1895.

Ter Haar, F., *De Matrimoniis Mixtis Eorumque Remediis*, Taurini-Romae: Marietti, 1931.

Thomassinus, L., *Vetus et Nova Ecclesiae Disciplina*, 10 vols., Mogentiaci, 1786-1787.

Uribé R. L., *De Episcoporum Ordinaria Dispensandi Facultate*, Medelii in Colombia: Typographia Bedout, 1939.

Van Hove, A., *Commentarium Louvaniense in Codicem Iuris Canonici*, Vol. I in 5, Mechliniae-Romae: Dessain. Tom. IV, *De Rescriptis*, 1936; Tom. V *De Privilegiis; De Dispensationibus*, 1939.

Vermeersch, A. Creusen, J., *Epitome Iuris Canonici*, 3 vols., Mechliniae-Romae: Dessain. Vol. I, 7. ed., 1949; Vol. II, 6. ed., 1940; Vol. III, 6. ed., 1946.

Vlaming, T., *Praelectiones Iuris Matrimonii ad Normam Juris Canonici*, 3. ed., 2 vols., Brussum in Hollandia: Sumptibus Editricis Anonymae olim Paulus Brand, 1919-1921.

Vromant, G., *Facultates Apostolicae*, 3. ed., Parisiis: Desclée de Bouwer, 1947.

Wernz, F. X., *Ius Decretalium*, 3. ed., 5 vols., Prati, 1913.

Wernz, F. X. Vidal, P., *Ius Canonicum*, 7 vols. in 8, Romae: apud Aedes Universitatis Gregorianae, Vol. I, 2. ed., 1952; Vol. II, 3. ed., 1943; Vol. III, 1933; Vol. IV, pars I, 1934, pars II, 1935; Vol. V, 3. ed., 1946; Vol. VI, 2. ed., 1949; Vol. VII, 2. ed., 1951.

Zitelli, Z., *De Dispensationibus Matrimonialibus*, Romae, 1887.

### Articles

Hannan, J. D., "Cases and Studies," *The Jurist*, VII (1947), 79-81.

MacKenzie, E., "Insufficient Canonical Causes for Matrimonial Dispensations," *The Jurist*, V (1945), 54-72.

Roelker, E., "Meaning of the Term 'Rationabilis'," *The Jurist*, IX (1949), 154-186.

———, "The Use of the Term 'Dispensatio' in the Code of Canon Law," *The Jurist*, X (1950), 138-151.

### Periodicals

*Apollinaris*, Romae, 1928-

*Ephemerides Theologicae Lovanienses*, Louvain, 1924-

*Jurist, The*, Washington, 1941-

## ABBREVIATIONS

*AAS*—*Acta Apostolicae Sedis*

*ASS*—*Acta Sancta Sedis*

*Fontes*—*Codicis Iuris Canonici Fontes . . . cura Gasparri editi*

Jaffé—*Regesta Pontificum Romanorum etc.*

Mansi—*Sacrorum Conciliorum Nova et Amplissima Collectio*

MPL—*Migne, Patrologiae Cursus Completus, Series Latina*

*S.R.R.*—*Sanctae Romanae Rotae Decisiones seu Sententiae*

## BIOGRAPHICAL NOTE

Stanislaus Joseph Kubik was born on March 28, 1918, in Wilbraham, Mass. After attending St. Mary's Parochial School in Indian Orchard, and Cathedral High School in Springfield, Mass., he enrolled at St. Charles' College in Catonsville, Md. In 1937 he entered the Seminary of Philosophy in Montreal, Canada, and completed his course of Theology at the Grand Seminary of Montreal, attaining a Licentiate of Sacred Theology. He was ordained for the Diocese of Springfield on June 19, 1943. He pursued graduate studies at the Grand Seminary, receiving the Doctorate of Sacred Theology in 1944. He was assigned as an assistant to St. Mary's Parish in Worcester, Mass., where he served for six years. When the diocese of Springfield was divided into the dioceses of Springfield and Worcester, he was automatically allocated to the new diocese of Worcester. In the fall of 1950 he enrolled in the School of Canon Law at the Catholic University of America, where he received the degree of Baccalaureate of Canon Law in June, 1951, and of Licentiate of Canon Law in June, 1952.

ALPHABETICAL INDEX

## CANON LAW STUDIES*

337. Bourque, Rev. John R., S.T.L., J.C.L., The judicial power of the Church—Canon 1553, § 1.
338. Cornell, Rev. Charles E., A.B., S.T.B., J.C.L., The juridical status of heretics and schismatics in good faith.
339. Fitzgerald, Rev. William Francis, A.B., S.T.L., J.C.L., The parish census and the *liber status animarum*.
340. Kubik, Rev. Stanislaus J., S.T.D., J.C.L., Invalidity of dispensations according to canon 84, § 1.
341. Nugent, Rev. John Gerard, C.M., J.C.L., Ordination in societies of the common life.
342. Peterson, Rev. Casimir Melvyn, S.S., A.B., S.T.L., J.C.L., Spiritual care in diocesan seminaries.
343. Reiss, Rev. John Charles, A.B., S.T.L., J.C.L., The time and place of sacred ordination.
344. Sheehan, Rev. Joseph George, J.C.L., The obligation of respect and obedience of clerics to their ordinary—Canon 127.
345. Shekleton, Rev. Matthew M., O.S.M., J.C.L., Doctrinal Interpretation of law.
346. Viau, Rev. Roger, S.T.L., J.C.L., Doubt in Canon Law.
347. Walsh, Rev. Donnell Anthony, A.B., J.C.L., The new law on secular institutes.

*For a complete list of the available numbers of this series apply to the Catholic University of America Press, 620 Michigan Avenue, N.E., Washington (17), D. C.

www.ingramcontent.com/pod-product-compliance
Lightning Source LLC
LaVergne TN
LVHW050201080826
844660LV00012B/327

* 9 7 8 0 8 1 3 2 2 5 0 9 8 *